W9-ACR-647

# Learn Korean with BTS (Bangtan Boys)

## The Fun, Effective Way to Learn Korean

Peter Kang

Learn Korean with BTS (Bangtan Boys)
Copyright © 2017 by Peter Kang

All rights reserved. No part of this book may be reproduced or transmitted in any form or by any means without written permission from the author.

ISBN-13: 978-1545164679
ISBN-10: 1545164673

Printed in USA by Createspace Publishing

# Dedication

To Kay

# Table of Contents

# Introduction

Who is BTS?

BTS (Bangtan Boys) debuted in 2013 with "No More Dream" and joined the battle of the Bs- B1A4, Block B, BAP, as well as competing against scores of other K-pop groups. Whereas the other groups have achieved local success, BTS has become world-wide and gained an enthusiastic, intense fandom (called A.R.M.Y.). In 2017, BTS has sold out arenas to fanatic A.R.M.Y.s in Brazil, Mexico, Chile, America, as well as the venues of Asia.

What is the reason for their frantic following? BTS has all the moves, synchronicity, artistry, lyricism of the best K-pop bands and then some. But, unlike the near complete silence on controversial topics found in K-pop, BTS writes about things that matter. In "No", they deliver a packed punch to the over-wrought festering education system that dominates life in Korea. With "No More Dream" they address the eternal generational battle of parents' and society's expectations versus the freedom youth want. In the anthemic "Not Today", BTS taps into themes of defying the powerful and standing your ground. Check out the music video, Koreans running in hijabs, toward what? And more importantly, what are they running from? Behind the music is a message of youthful empowerment rarely seen in K-pop.

How to Use This Book

This book was written for A.R.M.Y., K-pop fans, or those who are learning Korean. Recommended activities include getting on Youtube, reading and singing the lyrics, attending BTS concerts and joining in on the fan singing. Thousands have been inspired to learn Korean by K-pop, you may have been too.

This book is not intended to replace textbooks or study with more traditional books, but is intended to be a powerful and effective alternative or supplement. You can't help but upgrade your foreign language ability with songs by repeated listening and singing. Use the propulsive power of music to generate language. For listening, accent and pronunciation, songs are a lit, sui generis source for developing your skills.


Peter Kang

**The Korean Alphabet**

The Korean Alphabet (한글) Pronunciation

The Korean alphabet consists of 24 letters with 14 consonants and 10 vowels.
The 14 consonant letters are:

Consonants: ㄱ ㄴ ㄷ ㄹ ㅁ ㅂ ㅅ ㅇ ㅈ ㅊ ㅋ ㅌ ㅍ ㅎ
        g  n  d  l/f m  b  s  ng j  ch k  t  p  h

English sounds are represented by the letters under the Korean characters.
Note that ㅇ is silent and is pronounced ng as the ending on syllables.

Vowels: ㅏ ㅓ ㅗ ㅜ ㅡ ㅣ ㅑ ㅕ ㅛ ㅠ
    a  eo o  u  eu I  ya yeo yo yu

In addition there are compound letters - the digraphs.

5 double consonants: ㄲ ㄸ ㅃ ㅆ ㅉ
    kk tt pp ss jj

5 double vowels: ㅐ ㅒ ㅔ ㅖ ㅢ
    ae yae e ye ui

6 vowels and diphthongs with a w: ㅘ ㅙ ㅚ ㅝ ㅞ ㅟ
    wa wae oe wo we wi

The above English pronunciation analogs to the Korean alphabet are approximations and are only a loose guide. Preferably, the student should attempt to not use at all beyond the introduction/memorization period to the Korean alphabet.

There are many good webpages with audios of Korean alphabet pronunciation. An excellent one is Wikibooks at https://en.wikibooks.org/wiki/Korean/Alphabet.

One of the keen features of Korean is the what-you-see-is-what-you-hear nature of Korean spelling. Unlike English which can have several pronunications for a letter or two, Korean usually simply has one sound for one letter. This makes the learning of the phonics of Korean extremely simple and fast. You can be up and running with associations of sounds to letters in Korean with great accuracy in an hour or less.

The Korean Alphabet Scripting

Korean syllables are written with the pattern consonant+vowel, consonant+vowel+consonant, or consonant+vowel+consonant+consonant.

The vertically written vowels are to the right of the first consonant.

Example: ㄱ + ㅣ is written 기.

|   | ㅏ | ㅓ | ㅣ | ㅑ | ㅕ |
|---|---|---|---|---|---|
| ㄱ | 가 | 나 | 기 | 갸 | 겨 |
| ㄴ | 나 | 너 | 니 | 냐 | 녀 |
| ㄷ | 다 | 더 | 디 | 댜 | 뎌 |
| ㄹ | 라 | 러 | 리 | 랴 | 려 |
| ㅁ | 마 | 머 | 미 | 먀 | 며 |
| ㅂ | 바 | 버 | 비 | 뱌 | 벼 |
| ㅅ | 사 | 서 | 시 | 샤 | 셔 |
| ㅇ | 아 | 어 | 이 | 야 | 여 |
| ㅈ | 자 | 저 | 지 | 쟈 | 져 |
| ㅊ | 차 | 처 | 치 | 챠 | 쳐 |

| ㅋ | 카 | 커 | 키 | 캬 | 켜 |
| ㅌ | 타 | 터 | 티 | 탸 | 텨 |
| ㅂ | 바 | 버 | 비 | 뱌 | 벼 |

The horizontally written vowels are under the first consonant.

Example: ㄱ + ㅡ is written 그.

|   | ㅗ | ㅜ | ㅡ | ㅛ | ㅠ |
|---|---|---|---|---|---|
| ㄱ | 고 | 구 | 그 | 교 | 규 |
| ㄴ | 노 | 누 | 느 | 뇨 | 뉴 |
| ㄷ | 도 | 두 | 드 | 됴 | 듀 |
| ㄹ | 로 | 루 | 르 | 료 | 류 |
| ㅁ | 모 | 무 | 므 | 묘 | 뮤 |
| ㅂ | 보 | 부 | 브 | 뵤 | 뷰 |
| ㅅ | 소 | 수 | 스 | 쇼 | 슈 |
| ㅇ | 오 | 우 | 으 | 요 | 유 |
| ㅈ | 조 | 주 | 즈 | 죠 | 쥬 |
| ㅊ | 초 | 추 | 츠 | 쵸 | 츄 |
| ㅋ | 코 | 쿠 | 크 | 쿄 | 큐 |
| ㅌ | 토 | 투 | 트 | 툐 | 튜 |
| ㅂ | 보 | 부 | 브 | 뵤 | 뷰 |

When a third letter is added to the syllable, it is under the previous two letters.

Example: ㄱ + ㅏ + ㅁ is written 감, ㄱ + ㅗ + ㅁ is written 곰.

The fourth letter is written to the right of the bottom consonant.

Example: ㄱ + ㅏ + ㅂ + ㅅ is written 값. ㄱ + ㅡ + ㄹ + ㅁ is written 긂.

## Korean Basic Grammar

Korean is an agglutinative language, meaning the verb endings show tense, voice and formality.

The syntax is S-O-V. Subject-Object-Verb. This takes some adjusting to for English speakers and music is an excellent way to get accustomed to this difference.

Korean Tenses

The vast majority of K-Pop songs are written in the present tense and in the informal language. Korean has several layers of formal language. We will consider only the most common casual and formal styles.

*The Present Tense*

The dictionary verb is written with ~다.

Example: 가다 (to go), 오다 (to go), 가르치다 (to teach), 살다 (to live)

The most common formal present tense uses ~어요/아요 endings. Koreans will use this ending when talking to a stranger or an older person.

Verb stems ending with vowels ㅗ or ㅏ are followed by 아요.

Verb stems ending with vowels other than ㅗ or ㅏ are followed by 어요.

Drop the 다 to leave the stem and add the appropriate tense ending:

가다 → 가 + 요 → 가요 - go

있다 → 있 + 어요 → 있어요 - am/is/are

먹다 → 먹 + 어요 → 먹어요 - eat

마시다 → 마시 + 어요 → 마셔요 - drink

Note that 하다 (to do) changes to 해요.

The informal present ending uses ~어/여 or will simply drop 다 and the simple base verb will end the statement:

난 먹어. - I eat.

읽어 - read

K-Pop Example (Girls' Generation Express 999):

더 강한 커피가 **필요해**.

...**need** a stronger coffee.

The ending is informal present. The verb is 필요하다 meaning "to need". 다 is dropped. 하 from 하다 (to do) becomes 해. The formal ending would have been written 필요해요.

*The Past Tense*

The most common formal past tense endings are 았어요/었어요/였어요.

These are added to the verb stem. It's basically adding -ㅆ어요.

Verb stems ending with vowels ㅗ or ㅏ are followed by 았어요.

Verb stems ending with vowels other than ㅗ or ㅏ are followed by 었어요.

Verb stem 하 is followed by 였어요:

사다 - to buy. Verb stem 사

사 + 았어요 → 샀어요 - bought

오다 - to come. Verb stem 오

오 + 았어요 → 왔어요 - came

적다 - to write down. Verb stem 적

적 + 었어요 → 적었어요 (wrote)

하다 (to do). Verb stem 하

하 + 였어요 becomes 했어요 (did)

K-Pop Example (Girls' Generation Express 999):

선생님이 모자를 쓴 채 학교에 들어**갔어요**.

The teacher **went** to school while wearing a hat.


*The Future Tense*

A standard future tense in Korean adds ~ㄹ/을 거예요, which means "will" or "be going to".

Verb + ㄹ/을 거예요

1. Verb stems ending with a vowel (보다, 가다, 자다) add ㄹ 거예요.

2. Verb stems ending with a consonant (먹다, 찾다, 붙다) add 을 거예요.

3. Verb stems already ending with ㄹ at the end (놀다, 멀다, 살다) just add 거예요.

Examples:

가다 - to go

가 + ㄹ 거예요 → 갈 거예요 - will go

...지금 갈 거예요. - ...am/is/are going to go now.

...혼자 갈 거예요. - ...am/is/are going to go alone.

하다 - to do

하 + ㄹ 거예요 → 할 거예요. - will do

...뭐 할 거예요? - What am/is/are ...going to do?

...언제 할 거예요? - When am/is/are ...going to do?


입다 - to wear

입 + 을 거예요 → 입을 거예요. - will wear

...청바지 입을 거예요. - ...am/is/are going to wear blue jeans.

...티셔츠 입을 거예요. - ...am/is/are going to wear a t-shirt.


## Subject and Object Particles

*Subject Particles* ~는 / 은 and ~가 / 이

는/은 and 가/이 both are used as a subject marker.

는 and 가 are attached to words ending in vowels:

바다 + 는 → 바다는 - the sea

바다 + 가 → 바다가 - the sea

그녀 + 는 → 그녀는 - the girl

그녀 + 가 → 그녀가 - the girl


은 and 이 are attached to words ending in consonants:

밥 + 은 → 밥은 - the rice

밥 + 이 → 밥이 - the rice

책 + 은 → 책은 - the book

책 + 이 → 책이 - the book

However, 는/은 introduces a topic or a subject whereas 가/이 identifies a subject. The topic particle, 는/은, is used in cases when we make a general or factual statement whereas 가/이 is not.

Example:

비행기는 빠르다. - Planes are fast.

However, if you are a passenger in a plane and you are talking about your own plane compared to say faster planes. You might say:

비행기가 느리다 - (My) plane is slow.

So the identifier particle, 가/이, indicates a specific person or thing that the speaker and listener know or are aware of. In the example above, it is the plane that I am riding.

Another example:

바다는 푸르다. - The sea is blue. (A general statement)

However, suppose you see the sea at night and you may effuse:

바다가 까맣다! - The sea is black! (A particular statement)

K-Pop Example (2NE I Am The Best):

내가 제일 잘 나가. - I am the best.

내 + 가 = 내가 - I. I is the particular I. Don't confuse first 가 the second with the second 가. The second 가 is part of verb 나가 meaning "to go out".

*Object Particles ~을/를*

을 is used after a noun ending in a consonant:

옷 + 을 → 옷을 - clothes

를 is used after a noun ending in a vowel.

사과 + 를 → 사과를 - apple

Object words in Korean function similarly to object words in English:

...책을 읽었어요. - ...read a book.

...강을 건넜어요. - ...crossed a river.

K-Pop Example (2NE1 I Am The Best):

가치를 논하자면... - If...talking about my value...

가치를 - value

를 marks 가치 as the object. As the thing we are talking about.


Korean Syntax

The Korean language follows different structures and word orders than English. The big difference is that the verb always comes at the end of the Korean sentence, unlike in English. The following are the four basic Korean sentence structures. Note the abbreviations used in the explanation and the course of this book:

S-subject, N-noun, V-verb, A-adjective, O-object

1. S + N + V(to be).

나는 학생이다. - I am a student.

나는 - I, 학생 - student, 이다 - am

2. S + V. Subject + Verb

채영은 달린다. - Chae Young runs. (Chae Young- S, runs- V)

채영- Chae Young (a name)

은 (topic marker for Chae Young)

달린다 – run

3. S + A + V.

그는 정말 멍청해. - He is very stupid.

그는 – He

정말- very

멍청해 – stupid (literal English "does stupid")

채영은 정말 예쁘다. – Chae Young is very beautiful.

예쁘다 – beautiful

4. S + O + V. Subject + Object + Verb

나는 물을 마신다. – I drink water.

나는 – I

물을 – water

마신다 – drink

## *Danger*

## Lyrics/Translation/Notes

You in danger
You in danger
You in danger
You in danger

맨날 이런 식

You're always like this

맨날- always; 이런- this; 식- condition, order

너는 너 나는 나 너의 공식

You are you, I am me, your formula

N+의- (possessive tag); 공식- formula

핸드폰은 장식

My phone is just a mere accessory

장식- decoration, accessory

## 나 남친이 맞긴 하니?  I'm sick

I'm sick Am I really your boyfriend? I'm sick

남친- boyfriend; V+니- (question tag)

## 왜 숙제처럼 표현들을 미뤄

Why do you push off expressing your feelings like homework?

숙제- homework; N+처럼- like; 표현-expression; 미뤄- postpone

## 우리 무슨 Business? 아님 내가 싫어?

Are we in a business relationship? Or do you not like me?

무슨- which, what; 아님- if not, or; 싫어- don't like

## 덩 덩 디기 덩 덩

(Sound made when Korean drums are beaten)

## 좀 살가워져라 오늘도 또 주문을 빌어

Please be kinder, I'll request it again today

살갑다- to be affectionate; 오늘- today; 주문- order; 빌다- to beg

## 우린 평행선

We are parallel lines

평행선- parallel lines

## 같은 곳을 보지만 넘 다르지

We look at the same place but are so different

같은- alike; 곳- place; 보(지만)- look(but); 다르다- to be different

## 난 너밖에 없는데

I don't have anyone but you

밖에- outside of

## 왜 너 밖에 있는 것만 같은지

But why does it feel like I'm outside of you?

~지- (question form ending)

꽁하면 넌 물어 "삐쳤니?"

If I stay quiet, you ask, "Are you mad?"

물어- ask; 삐쳤니- are you mad(sulking)?

날 삐치게 했던 적이나 있었니?

Well, did you even pretend to make me mad?

적하다- to pretend

넌 귀요미 난 지못미

You're a cutie and I am pitiful

귀요미- cutie; 지못미- pitiful person

생기길 니가 더 사랑하는 기적이

I hope for a miracle of you loving me more than I love you

생기길 – creative path; 사랑-love; 기적- miracle

넌 내가 없는데 난 너로 가득해

You don't have me but I'm filled with you

없는데- lacking, without


미칠 것 같아 Whoa

whoa It's driving me crazy

미치다- to go mad, crazy


근데 왜 이러는데 왜 바보 만들어

Then, why are you doing this? Why are you making me into a fool?

근데- then; 이러는데- this; 바보- a fool; 만들다- to make

나 이제 경고해 헷갈리게 하지 마

I'm warning you now, stop confusing me

이제- now; 경고해- warn; 헷갈리게- confuse; 하지 마- don't

장난해 너? 도대체 내가 뭐야?

Are you joking? What am I to you?

장난해- fool, toy with; 도대체- indeed

만만해 Uh? 날 갖고 노는 거야?

Am I easy to you? Are you playing with me?

만만해 – trifle with; 갖고- take; 노는- playful; 거야- thing

너 지금 위험해 왜 나를 시험해?

You're in danger right now, why are you testing me?

위험해- endanger; 시험해- test

왜 나를 시험해? 헷갈리게 하지 마

Why are you testing me? Stop confusing me

장난해 너? 도대체 내가 뭐야?

Are you joking? What am I to you?

만만해 Uh? 날 갖고 노는 거야?

Am I easy to you? Are you playing with me?

너 지금 위험해 왜 나를 시험해?

You're in danger right now, why are you testing me?

왜 나를 시험해? 헷갈리게 하지 마

Why are you testing me? Stop confusing me

너 땜에 너무 아파

It hurts so much because of you

땜에- because of; 아파- hurt

너 땜에 너무 아파

It hurts so much because of you

너 땜에 너무 아파

It hurts so much because of you

헷갈리게 하지 마

Stop confusing me

헷갈리다- to confuse; 하지 마- don't do

너 내게 너무 나빠

You're so bad to me

너- you; 내게- to me; 너무- so, too; 나빠- bad

너 내게 너무 나빠

You're so bad to me

너 내게 너무 나빠

You're so bad to me

헷갈리게 하지 마

Stop confusing me

연락 부재중 Unlock 수배 중

You're not answering, I'm looking for how to unlock you

부재중- absence; 수배 중- wanting

너란 여자 본심을 수색 중

I'm investigating a girl like you and your true feelings

~란/랑- with; 여자- girl; 본심- true feeling; 수색 – investigation; 중- during

고작 보내 준 게 문자 두세 줄

All you send me is a line or two through text

고작- only; 보내- send; 준- given; 게- it, thing; 문자- text, letter; 두- two; 세- three

이게 내가 바랬던 연애 꿈?

Is this the relationship and dream that I've wanted?

바랬던- hoped for; 연애- relationship; 꿈- dream

파란만장 Love story 다 어디 갔나?

Where did my exciting love story go?

파란만장- blue ups and downs(thrilling)

Drama 에 나온 주인공들 다 저리 가라

Move out of the way, drama characters

주인공- actors, characters; 들- (plural tag); 저리- there

너 때문에 수백 번 쥐어 잡는 머리카락

I rip out my hair hundreds of times because of you

수백- hundreds; 번- times; 쥐어 잡는- grab and pull out; 머리카락- hair

너 담담 그저 당당 날 차 빵빵

But you don't care, you think it's fine and you kick me (lit. You're calm, just confident, me a car pang, pang)

담담- calm; 그저- just; 당당- confident; 차- car

뭐니 뭐니 난 네게 뭐니?

What, what, what am I to you?

뭐니- what?

너보다 니 친구에게 전해 듣는 소식

I hear about you from your friends rather than you

-보다- than; 전해- transmit; 소식- news

원해 원해 Huh 너를 원해

I want you, I want you, huh, I want you

원해- want

너란 여잔 사기꾼 내 맘을 흔든 범인

A girl like you, a con-artist, a criminal who shook my heart

사기꾼- con artist, fraud; 흔든- shaken; 범인- criminal

불이 붙기 전부터 내 맘 다 쓰고

You used up my heart before the fire even started

전- before; -부터- from; 쓰다- to use

일방적인 구애들 해 봤자 헛수고

I can try to have a one-sided relationship but it'll be useless

일방적인- one sided; 구애들- lovers; 해 봤자- try; 헛수고- useless

너에게 난 그저 연인이 아닌 우정이 편했을지도 몰라 I'm a love loser

Maybe you're more comfortable with being friends instead of lovers, I'm a love loser

연인- lovers; 아닌- not; 우정- friendship; 편하다- to be comfortable

넌 내가 없는데 난 너로 가득해

You don't have me but I'm filled with you

미칠 것 같아 Whoa whoa

It's driving me crazy Whoa whoa

근데 왜 이러는데 왜 바보 만들어

Why are you doing this? Why are you making me into a fool?

나 이제 경고해 헷갈리게 하지 마

I'm warning you now, stop confusing me

장난해 너? 도대체 내가 뭐야?

Are you joking? What am I to you?

만만해 Uh? 날 갖고 노는 거야?

Am I easy to you? Are you playing with me?

너 지금 위험해 왜 나를 시험해?

You're in danger right now, why are you testing me?

왜 나를 시험해? 헷갈리게 하지 마

Why are you testing me? Stop confusing me

장난해 너? 도대체 내가 뭐야?

Are you joking? What am I to you?

만만해 Uh? 날 갖고 노는 거야?

Am I easy to you? Are you playing with me?

너 지금 위험해 왜 나를 시험해?

You're in danger right now, why are you testing me?

왜 나를 시험해? 헷갈리게 하지 마

Why are you testing me? Stop confusing me


너 땜에 너무 아파

It hurts so much because of you

너 땜에 너무 아파

It hurts so much because of you

너 땜에 너무 아파

It hurts so much because of you


헷갈리게 하지 마

Stop confusing me

너 내게 너무 나빠

You're so bad to me

너 내게 너무 나빠

You're so bad to me

너 내게 너무 나빠

You're so bad to me

헷갈리게 하지 마

Stop confusing me

## *Not Today*

**Lyrics/Translation/Notes**

All the underdogs in the world
A day may come when we lose
But it is not today
Today we fight!
No not today

언젠가 꽃은 지겠지

Some day, the flowers will wither

언젠가- sometime; 지나다- to pass by

But no not today

그 때가 오늘은 아니지

But today's not the day

그- that; 때- time

No no not today

아직은 죽기엔

It's too early to die

아직- still, 죽기엔- to die

Too good day
No no not today
No no no not today

그래 우리는 extra

Yeah, we are extra

그래- right, yeah

But still part of this world
Extra plus ordinary

그것도 별 거 아녀

That's not even that special

그것- that; 도- too, even

오늘은 절대 죽지 말아

Today we'll never die

절대- absolutely; 죽다- to die; 말아- not

빛은 어둠을 뚫고 나가

The light will pierce through the darkness

빛- light; 어둠- darkness; 뚫(고)- pierce(and); 나가- go out

새 세상 너도 원해

You want a new world too

새- new; 세상- world; 너- you; 원하다- to want

Oh baby yes I want it

날아갈 수 없음 뛰어

If you can't fly, run

날다- to fly; ~수 있다- can; 없음- not having; 뛰어- run

Today we will survive

뛰어갈 수 없음 걸어

If you can't run, walk

뛰다- to run; 걷다- to walk

Today we will survive

걸어갈 수 없음 기어

Even if you have to crawl, gear up
If you can't walk, crawl

기다- crawl

기어서라도 gear up

gears too, gear up

겨눠 총! 조준! 발사!

Point, aim, shoot!

Not not today! Not not today!

Hey 뱁새들아 다 hands up

Hey crow-tits, everyone, hands up

뱁새들아- crow-tit (small bird)

Hey 친구들아 다 hands up

Hey friends, hands up

Hey 나를 믿는다면 hands up

Hey, if you trust me, hands up

믿는다- to believe;~면- if

총! 조준! 발사!

Point, aim, shoot!

죽지 않아 묻지 마라

We won't die, don't ask

묻다- to believe; 마라- don't

소리 질러 not not today

Scream, not not today

꿇지 마라 울지 않아

Don't kneel, we won't cry

손을 들어 not not today

Hands up, not not today
Hey not not today
Hey not not today
Hey not not today

총! 조준! 발사!

Point, aim, shoot!


Too hot 성공을 doublin'

Too hot, success doublin'

Too hot 차트를 덤블링

Too hot, somersaulting on the charts

Too high we on 트램펄린

Too high, we on trampoline

Too high 누가 좀 멈추길

Too high, someone stop us

멈추다- to stop


우린 할 수가 없었단다 실패

We couldn't fail

우린 (우리는)- we; 실패- failure

서로가 서롤 전부 믿었기에

Because we believed in each other

서로- each other; 전부- enough; 믿다- to believe; 었- (past tag);

~기에- because

What you say yeah (say yeah)
Not today yeah (day yeah)
오늘은 안 죽어 절대 yeah

We won't die today yeah

안- not

너의 곁에 나를 믿어

Trust me, who is next to you

너의- your; 곁(에)- side(at)

Together we won't die

나의 곁에 너를 믿어

I trust you, who is next to me
Together we won't die

함께라는 말을 믿어

We believe in the word, together

함께- together; 말- word, speech

방탄이란 걸 믿어 (믿어)

We believe that we're Bangtan

걸- thing, that

겨눠 총! 조준! 발사!

Point, aim, shoot!


Not not today! Not not today!

Hey 뱁새들아 다 hands up

Hey crow-tits, everyone, hands up

Hey 친구들아 다 hands up

Hey friends, hands up

Hey 나를 믿는다면 hands up

Hey, if you trust me, hands up

총! 조준! 발사!

Point, aim, shoot!


죽지 않아 묻지 마라

We won't die, don't ask

소리 질러 not not today

Scream, not not today

꿇지 마라 울지 않아

Don't kneel, we won't cry

손을 들어 not not today

Hands up, not not today

Hey not not today

Hey not not today

Hey not not today

총! 조준! 발사!

Point, aim, shoot!

Throw it up! Throw it up!

니 눈 속의 두려움 따위는 버려

Throw away the fear in your eyes

니 눈- eye; 속의- in; 두려움- fear; 따위- etc, and the like 버려

Break it up! Break it up!

널 가두는 유리천장 따윈 부숴

Break the glass ceiling that traps you

가두는- trapping; 유리천장- glass ceiling; 부숴- break

Turn it up! (turn it up!)

Burn it up! (burn it up!)

승리의 날까지 (fight!)

Till the day of victory (fight!)

승리- victory; 날-day; ~까지- until

무릎 꿇지 마 무너지지마

Don't kneel, don't break down

무릎- knee; 꿇다-drop down; 마- don't; 무너지다- to collapse

That's (do) not today!

Not not today! Not not today!

Hey 뱁새들아 다 hands up

Hey crow-tits, everyone, hands up

Hey 친구들아 다 hands up

Hey friends, hands up

Hey 나를 믿는다면 hands up

Hey, if you trust me, hands up

총! 조준! 발사!

Point, aim, shoot!

죽지 않아 묻지 마라

We won't die, don't ask

소리 질러 not not today

Scream, not not today

꿇지 마라 울지 않아

Don't kneel, we won't cry

손을 들어 not not today

Hands up, not not today

Hey not not today

Hey not not today

Hey not not today

총! 조준! 발사!

Point, aim, shoot!

## *Spring Day*

**Lyrics/Translation/Notes**

보고 싶다 이렇게

I miss you

보고 싶다- want to see ; 이렇게- like this

말하니까 더 보고 싶다

Saying this makes me miss you
even more

말하다- to speak; ~니까- because

말하니까 더 보고 싶다

너희 사진을 보고 있어도 보고 싶다

Even when I'm looking at a picture of you
I miss you

너희- your; 사진- picture

너무 야속한 시간

Time's so cruel

야속한- cruel

## 나는 우리가 밉다

I hate us

밉다- to hate

## 이젠 얼굴 한 번 보는 것도

## 힘들어진 우리가

Even seeing each other for once
Is now so hard between us

이젠- now; 얼굴- face; 한 번- one time; 보는 것도

힘들어진- becoming


## 여긴 온통 겨울 뿐이야

It's all winter here

여긴- here; 온통- complete; 겨울- winter; 뿐이(야)- only(emphatic tag)

## 8 월에도 겨울이 와

Even in August

와- come

## 마음은 시간을 달려가네

My heart is running on time

마음- heart; 달려가네- run and go

## 홀로 남은 설국열차

Alone on the Snowpiercer

홀로- alone; 남은- remaining; 설국열차- snow country train

## 니 손 잡고 지구 반대편까지 가

I want to get to the other side
Holding your hand

## 겨울을 끝내고파

I want to put an end to this winter

끝내다- to end

그리움들이

How much longings

그리움- longing

얼마나 눈처럼 내려야

Do we have to see falling like snow

얼마나- how much; 눈- snow; ~처럼- like, as if

그 봄날이 올까

For that spring day to come

봄- spring; 날- day; 올까 (온다)- will come (to come)

Friend

작은 먼지처럼

Like the tiny dust

작은- small, tiny; 먼지- dust

작은 먼지처럼

Like the tiny dust

허공을 떠도는

Floating in the air

허공- void

날리는 눈이 나라면

If I was the snow in the air

날리는- floating, flying

조금 더 빨리 네게닿을 수 있을 텐데

I would be able to get to you just a little faster

조금- little; 더- more; 빨리- fast; 네게닿- reach you, touch you; ~수 있을

텐데- would

눈꽃이 떨어져요

Snowflakes fall down

눈(꽃)- snow(flower), snowflakes

또 조금씩 멀어져요

And get farther away little by little

조금씩- bit by bit, little by little; 멀어져요- become farther

보고 싶다 (보고 싶다)

I miss you (I miss you)

보고 싶다 (보고 싶다)

I miss you (I miss you)

얼마나 기다려야

How much longer do I have to wait

기다려(야)- wait (should)

또 몇 밤을 더 새워야

How many more nights do I have to stay awake

몇- how many; 새워야- should stay awake

널 보게 될까 (널 보게 될까)

To see you (to see you)

될까- would be, would be good

만나게 될까 (만나게 될까)

To meet you (to see you)

만나다- to meet


추운 겨울 끝을 지나

Passing by the edge of the cold winter

추운- cold; 끝- end, edge; 지나- pass

다시 봄날이 올 때까지

Until the spring days come again

꽃 피울 때까지

Until flowers blossom

피다- to bloom

그곳에 좀 더 머물러줘, 머물러줘

Stay in that place just a little bit longer, Stay

그곳에- there; 좀- a little; 머물다- stay; ~줘- give

니가 변한 건지

Is it you who changed

변한- changed; 건- it

(니가 변한 건지)

(Is it you who changed)

(아니면 내가 변한 건지)

Or is it me

아니면- if not

아니면 내가 변한 건지

(Or is it me)

이 순간 흐르는 시간조차 미워

I hate the time flowing in this moment

이- this; 순간- moment; 흐르는- flowing; -조차- in the process, as; 미워- hate

우리가 변한 거지 뭐

Well, I guess we just changed

뭐- what

그래 밉다 니가

That's right, I hate you

넌 떠났지만 모두가 그런 거지 뭐

Just like how everyone changes

떠나다- to leave; ~지만- but; 모두 -all; 그런- like that

단 하루도 너를 잊은 적이 없었지 난

Even though you left me Not a day passed
Where I didn't think about you

잊은- forgetting; 적이- occurence

솔직히 보고 싶은데

Honestly I miss you

솔직히- honestly, candidly; 싶은데- want

이만 너를 지울게

But I'll erase you

지울게- erasure

그게 널 원망하기보단 덜 아프니까

Because it hurts less than to blame you

원망- resentment; 보단- than; 덜- less; 아프다- to hurt

시린 널 불어내 본다

In pain, I try to exhale you

시린- painful; 불어내- exhale

연기처럼 하얀 연기처럼

Like smoke, like white smoke

연기- smoke; 하얀- white

말로는 지운다 해도 사실 난 아직 널 보내지 못하는데

I say that I'll erase you, but the truth is that I can't let you go yet

말로는- Saying; 사실- truth; 보내지- send; 못하다- can't

눈꽃이 떨어져요

Snowflakes fall down

또 조금씩 멀어져요

And get farther away little by little

보고 싶다 (보고 싶다)

I miss you (I miss you)

보고 싶다 (보고 싶다)

I miss you (I miss you)

얼마나 기다려야

How much longer do I have to wait

또 몇 밤을 더 새워야

How many more nights do I have to stay awake

널 보게 될까 (널 보게 될까)

To see you (to see you)

만나게 될까 (만나게 될까)

To meet you (to see you)

You know it all
You're my best friend

아침은 다시 올 거야

The morning will come again

어떤 어둠도 어떤 계절도 영원할 순 없으니까

Because no darkness or season Can last forever

영원- eternity, forever

벚꽃이 피나봐요

I guess cherry blossoms are blooming

벚꽃- cherry blossom

이 겨울도 끝이 나요

I wonder, is this winter ending too?

보고 싶다 (보고 싶다)

I miss you (I miss you)

보고 싶다 (보고 싶다)

I miss you (I miss you)

조금만 기다리면

If you wait just a little bit more

며칠 밤만 더 새우면

If you stay awake for just a few more nights

만나러 갈게 (만나러 갈게)

I'll go to meet you (I'll go there to meet you)

데리러 갈게 (데리러 갈게)

I'll come to get you (I'll come to get you)


추운 겨울 끝을 지나

Passing by the edge of the cold winter

다시 봄날이 올 때까지

Until the spring days come again

꽃 피울 때까지 Until flowers blossom

그곳에 좀 더 머물러줘

Stay in that place just a little bit longer

머물러줘 Stay

## *Blood, Sweat and Tears*

**Lyrics/Translation/Notes**

내 피 땀 눈물

My blood, sweat and tears

내- my

내 마지막 춤을

My last dance

마지막- final, end, last; 춤- dance

다 가져가 가

Go take it all away

다- all; 가져가- take

내 피 땀 눈물

My blood, sweat and tears

내 차가운 숨을

My cold breath

차가운- cold; 숨- breath

다 가져가 가

Go take it all away

내 피 땀 눈물

My blood, sweat and tears

내 피 땀 눈물도

Even my blood, sweat and tears

~도- too, even

내 몸 마음 영혼도

Even my body, heart and soul

너의 것인 걸 잘 알고 있어

I know that it's all yours

너의- your; 걸- thing; 잘- well; 알고 있어- would know

이건 나를 벌받게 할 주문

This is a spell that'll punish me

이건- this; 나-me; 벌-punishment; 받게- receiving; 할- (future form of 하다);

주문- order

Peaches and cream
Sweeter than sweet
Chocolate cheeks
And chocolate wings

But 너의 날개는 악마의 것

But your wings are wings of the devil

날개- wings; 악마- devil; ~의- (possessive marker)

너의 그 sweet 앞엔 bitter bitter

In front of your sweet is bitter bitter

Kiss me 아파도 돼

Kiss me, I don't care if it hurts,

Your whiskey, deep into my throat

아파- hurting

어서 날 조여줘

더 이상 아플 수도 없게

Hurry and choke me

어서- hurry; 조여- choke; 이상- more

Baby 취해도 돼 이제 널 들이켜

Baby, I don't care if I get drunk, I'll drink you in now

Baby 취해- drunk; 돼- okay; 들이켜- take in, bring, tug

목 깊숙이 너란 위스키

So I can't hurt any more

목- throat; 깊숙이- deeply; 너란- with you; 위스키- whiskey

내 피 땀 눈물

My blood, sweat and tears

내 마지막 춤을

My last dance

다 가져가 가

Take it away

내 피 땀 눈물

My blood, sweat and tears

내 차가운 숨을

My cold breath

다 가져가 가

Take it away

원해 많이 많이 많이 많이

I want you a lot, a lot, a lot

원해 많이 많이 많이 많이 많이 많이

I want you a lot, a lot, a lot

원하다- to want

원해 많이 많이 많이 많이

I want you a lot, a lot, a lot

원해 많이 많이 많이 많이 많이 많이

I want you a lot, a lot, a lot

아파도 돼 날 묶어줘

I don't care if it hurts, tie me up

묶어- tie up

내가 도망칠 수 없게

So I won't be able to run away

도망하다- to escape

꽉 쥐고 날 흔들어줘

Grab me tightly and shake me

꽉- completely, very; 쥐다- hold; 흔들다- to shake

내가 정신 못 차리게

So I can't snap out of it

정신- mind, consciousness; 차리게- clarity

Kiss me on the lips lips

둘만의 비밀

Our own little secret

둘(만)- two(only); 비밀- secret

너란 감옥에 중독돼 깊이

I wanna be addicted to your prison

감옥(에)- prison(to, in); 중독(돼)- addiction(become); 깊이- deeply

니가 아닌 다른 사람 섬기지 못해

So I can't serve anyone that's not you

다른- other; 사람- person; 섬기지- serve

알면서도 삼켜버린 독이 든 성배

Even though I know, I drink the poisonous Holy Grail

알면서도- even if I know; 삼켜- drink; 버린- wasted; 독- poison; ~든- put in

성배- Holy Grail


내 피 땀 눈물

My blood, sweat and tears

내 마지막 춤을

My last dance

다 가져가 가

Take it away

내 피 땀 눈물

My blood, sweat and tears

내 차가운 숨을

My cold breath

다 가져가 가

Take it away


원해 많이 많이 많이 많이

I want you a lot, a lot, a lot

원해 많이 많이 많이 많이 많이 많이

I want you a lot, a lot, a lot

원해 많이 많이 많이 많이

I want you a lot, a lot, a lot

원해 많이 많이 많이 많이 많이 많이

I want you a lot, a lot, a lot

나를 부드럽게 죽여줘

Kill me softly

부드럽게- softly; 줘- give

너의 손길로 눈 감겨줘

Close my eyes with your touch

손길(로)- touch, point(thru); 감겨- close

어차피 거부할 수조차 없어

I can't even reject you anyway

어차피- regardless, anyway; 거부- refuse; ~조차- process

더는 도망갈 수조차 없어

I can't run away anymore

니가 너무 달콤해 너무 달콤해

You're too sweet, too sweet

달콤하다- to be sweet

너무 달콤해서

Because you're too sweet

He too was a tempter. He too was linked to second. The evil world with which I no longer want to have anything to do

내 피 땀 눈물

My blood, sweat and tears

내 피 땀 눈물

My blood, sweat and tears

# *Fire*

## Lyrics/Translation/Notes

불타오르네

It's on fire

불타- burning fire; 오르네- comes


Fire Fire Fire Fire


When I wake up in my room 난 뭣도 없지

When I wake up in my room, I have nothing

해가 지고 난 후 비틀대며 걷지

After the sun sets, I sway as I walk

해- sun; 지다- to lose, set; 후- after; 비틀대(며)- sway(and); 걷다- to walk

다 만신창이로 취했어 취했어

With all my heart- drunk, drunk

다- all; 만신창이로- world heart

막 욕해 길에서 길에서

I'm swearing from the streets

막- just; 욕해- curse; 길- street; ~에서- from


나 맛이 갔지 미친놈 같지

I've lost it, I'm like a crazy guy

맛이- taste; 갔지- gone; 미친놈- crazy jerk; 같지- as, like

다 엉망진창, livin' like 삐-이-

Everything's a mess, livin' like

엉망진창- mess

Fire Fire Fire Fire


니 멋대로 살어 어차피 니 꺼야

Live however you want, it's yours anyway

멋대로- as if can't be helped; 살어- live; 니 꺼야- yours

Say La la la la la (La la la la la)

애쓰지 좀 말어 져도 괜찮아

Stop trying a little, it's okay to lose

애쓰지- try; 좀 말어- stop, end some; 져도- even losing; 괜찮아- is okay


Errbody say La la la la la (La la la la la)
Say La la la la la (La la la la la)

손을 들어 소리질러 Burn it up

Throw your hands up, scream, burn it up

손- hand; 들어- raise; 소리질러- scream


불타오르네

It's on fire
(Eh eh oh eh oh)

싹 다 불태워라 Bow wow wow

Set everything on fire, bow wow wow

싹- entirely, completely

싹 다 불태워라 Bow wow wow

 (Eh eh oh eh oh)
Set everything on fire, bow wow wow


Hey, burn it up 전부 다

Hey, burn it up, all of it

태울 것 같이

Hey, turn it up 새벽이 다 갈 때까지

Hey, turn it up, until the dawn is gone

새벽- sunrise, dawn

그냥 살아도 돼 우린 젊기에

Just live because we're young

그냥- just; 젊기에- because of youth

그 말하는 넌 뭔 수저길래

Who are you to compare me with others?

말하는- speaking; 수저- spoon, chopsticks (idiomatic for manners)

수저수저 거려 난 사람인데

I'm only human

수저수저 거려 난 사람인데

거려- choose


(So what~)


니 멋대로 살어 어차피 니 꺼야

Live however you want, it's yours anyway

애쓰지 좀 말어 져도 괜찮아

Stop trying, it's okay to lose
Errbody say La la la la la (La la la la la)
Say La la la la la (La la la la la)

손을 들어 소리질러 Burn it up

Throw your hands up, scream, burn it up

불타오르네

It's on fire

(Eh eh oh eh oh)

싹 다 불태워라 Bow wow wow

Set everything on fire, bow wow wow
(Eh eh oh eh oh)

싹 다 불태워라 Bow wow wow

Set everything on fire, bow wow wow

(Fire) 겁 많은 자여 여기로(Fire)

All you with a lot of fear, come here

겁- fear; 많은- much, many; 자여- people; 여기- hear

(Fire) [진/정] 괴로운 자여 여기로(Fire)

All you who are suffering, come here

괴로운- suffering

(Fire) [진/정] 맨주먹을 들고 All night long(Fire)

Lift up your fists, all night long

맨주먹- bare fists; 들고- hold up

(Fire) 진군하는 발걸음으로

(Fire) With marching footsteps (Fire) Run and go crazy

진군하는- allied, marching; 발걸음(으로)- steps(thru)

(Fire) 뛰어봐 미쳐버려 다

Try and run crazy throw it all away

---

52

<u>싹 다 불태워라</u> Bow wow wow

Set everything on fire, bow wow wow

<u>싹 다 불태워라</u> Bow wow wow

Set everything on fire, bow wow wow

<u>(Fire Fire)</u>

<u>싹 다 불태워라</u> Bow wow wow

Set everything on fire, bow wow wow
<u>(Fire Fire)</u>

<u>싹 다 불태워라</u> Bow wow wow

Set everything on fire, bow wow wow

<u>싹 다 불태워라</u> Bow wow wow

Set everything on fire, bow wow wow

<u>용서해줄게</u>

I'll forgive you

# *Save Me*

## Lyrics/Translation/Notes

난 숨쉬고 싶어 이 밤이 싫어
I want to breathe, I hate this night
Don't wanna be lonely
Just wanna be yours
숨쉬다- to breathe; ~고- and; 밤- night; 싫어- dislike, hate

이젠 깨고 싶어 꿈속이 싫어
I want to wake up, I hate this dream
깨다- to wake up

내 안에 갇혀서 난 죽어있어
I'm trapped inside of myself and I'm dead
안에- inside; 갇혀서- trapped; 죽어있어- dead
Don't wanna be lonely
Just wanna be yours

왜 이리 깜깜한 건지 니가 없는 이 곳은
Why is it so dark where you're not here
왜- why; 이리- here; 깜깜한- dark; 건지- thing, ~ness

위험하잖아 망가진 내 모습
It's dangerous how wrecked I am

54

위험- danger; 하잖아- you know; 망가진- wrecked; 모습- appearance
구해줘 날 나도 날 잡을 수 없어
Save me because I can't get a grip on myself
구하다- to save; 잡을 수 없어- can't hold, grip
내 심장소릴 들어봐
Try listening to my heartbeat
심장- heart; 소리-sound; 들어(봐)- listen(try)

심장소릴 들어봐
Try listening to my heartbeat
제멋대로 널 부르잖아
It calls you whenever you want
제멋대로- through you; 부르(잖아)- calls(as you know)
이 까만 어둠 속에서
Because within this pitch black darkness
까만- complete; 어둠- darkness
너는 이렇게 빛나니까
Because you shine this way
이렇게- like this; 빛나(니까)- shine(because)

그 손을 내밀어줘 save me save me
Give me your hand save me save me
내밀어줘- hold out and give
I need your love before I fall, fall
그 손을 내밀어줘 save me save me
Give me your hand save me save me
I need your love before I fall, fall
그 손을 내밀어줘 save me save me
Give me your hand save me save me
그 손을 내밀어줘 save me save me
Give me your hand save me save me

Save me, save me

오늘따라 달이 빛나
Today the moon shines brighter
오늘(따라)- (as)today; 달이- moon; 빛나- shines

내 기억 속의 빈칸
on the blank spot in my memories

55

기억- memory; 빈칸- blank space

날 삼켜버린 이 lunatic,
It swallowed me, this lunatic,
삼켜(버린)-swallowed(away)
please save me tonight
(Please save me tonight,
please save me tonight)
이 치기 어린 광기 속
This stroke inside a childish madness
치기- stroke; 어린- child; 광기- madness

이 치기 어린 광기 속
This stroke inside a childish madness
나를 구원해줄 이 밤
you will save me tonight
구원해(줄)- save(will give)

난 알았지 너란 구원이
I knew that your salvation
알았지- knew; 너란- with you; 구원이- salvation
내 삶의 일부며 아픔을
My life's part and suffering
삶(의)- life('s); 일부-part; 아픔- hurt, suffering
감싸줄 유일한 손길
given an appreciating aiding gesture
감쌈- appreciation; 유일- help; 손길- gesture
The best of me,
난 너밖에 없지
you're the only thing I have
너(밖에)- you(besides)
나 다시 웃을 수 있도록
So I can laugh again
다시- again; 웃을 수 있도록
더 높여줘 니 목소릴
Raise my voice higher
높여- raise
Play on
내 심장소릴 들어봐
Try listening to my heartbeat
제멋대로 널 부르잖아

It calls you whenever you want
이 까만 어둠 속에서
Because within this pitch black darkness,
너는 이렇게 빛나니까
Because you shine this way


그 손을 내밀어줘 save me save me
Give me your hand save me save me
I need your love before I fall, fall
I need your love before I fall, fall
그 손을 내밀어줘 save me save me
Give me your hand save me save me
I need your love before I fall, fall
그 손을 내밀어줘 save me save me
Give me your hand save me save me
그 손을 내밀어줘 save me save me
Give me your hand save me save me


고마워 내가 나이게 해줘서
Thank you for helping me be me
고마워- thanks
이 내가 날게 해줘서
I need your love before I fall, fall
이런 내게 날갤 줘서
For helping me fly
날갤- flight; 줘(서)-(for)giving
꼬깃하던 날 개 줘서
For giving me wings
답답하던 날 깨줘서
For straightening me out
답답하던- frustrasted; 날- day; 깨줘서- broken
꿈 속에만 살던 날 깨워줘서
For breaking the life only in dreams
~만- only; 살던- lived


널 생각하면 날 개어서
For waking me from doubtful days of you
생각하다- to think; ~면- if

LEARN KOREAN WITH BTS

슬픔 따윈 나 개줬어
The sad things I broke
(Thank you. '우리'가 돼 줘서)
(Thank you. For giving us 'we')


그 손을 내밀어줘 save me save me
Give me your hand save me save me
I need your love before I fall, fall
I need your love before I fall, fall
그 손을 내밀어줘 save me save me
Give me your hand save me save me
I need your love before I fall, fall

# *Run*

## Lyrics/Translation/Notes

넌 내 하나뿐인 태양 세상에 딱 하나
You are my only sun, one and only in the world
하나뿐인- only one; 태양- sun; 딱- just

널 향해 피었지만 난 자꾸 목말라
I bloomed for you, but I'm still getting thirsty
향해- direction; 피었(지만)-bloomed(but); 자꾸- often; 목말라- thirsty

너무 늦었어 늦었어 너 없이 살 순 없어
It's too late, too late, I can't live without you
너무- too; 늦었어- late

가지가 말라도 더 힘껏 손을 뻗어
Though my branch runs dry, I reach for you with all my strength
가지- branch; 말라-dry; 힘껏- all strength; 뻗어- reach, extend

손 뻗어봤자 금세
As I urgently reach
금세- fast

깨버릴 꿈 꿈 꿈
It is just an broken dream dream dream
깨버릴- busted, broken

미칠 듯 달려도
No matter that I run like crazy
미칠- crazy; 듯- meaning; like 달려가다- to run

또 제자리일 뿐 뿐 뿐
I remain on the same place place place
제자리일- my place, same place

그냥 날 태워줘 그래 더 밀쳐내줘
Just burn me! Yes, push me out!
그냥- just; 태워줘- burn me; 그래- yes, indeed; 밀쳐내줘- push out

이건 사랑에 미친 멍청이의 뜀박질
This is crazy-fool's love running
멍청이- fool; 뜀박질- running


더 뛰게 해줘
Let me run more
뛰게- run

나를 더 뛰게 해줘
Please let me run more

두 발에 상처만 가득해도
Even though my feet are full of scars
두- two; 발- feet; 상처- injury; 가득하다- to be full

니 얼굴만 보면 웃는 나니까
I smile whenever I see you
얼굴-face; 보(면)- see(if); 웃는- smiling; 나(니까)-happen(because)


다시 Run Run Run 난 멈출 수가 없어
Let's run run run again! I can't stop running
멈출 수가 없어- can't stop

또 Run Run Run 난 어쩔 수가 없어
Let's run run run again! I can't help it.

어차피 이것밖에 난 못해
Anyhow, I can't do anything else.

너를 사랑하는 것 밖엔 못해
I can't help loving you.
사랑하는- loving; 밖엔- besides


다시 Run Run Run 넘어져도 괜찮아
Let's run run run again! It's ok to fall down
넘어지다- to fall; 괜찮아- it's okay

또 Run Run Run 좀 다쳐도 괜찮아
Let's run run run again! It's ok to be injured
좀- a little, some; 다쳐(도)- injure(even)
가질 수 없다 해도 난 족해
I am happy enough even though I can't get you
가질 수 없다- can't get; 족해- is good enough
바보 같은 운명아 나를 욕해
Curse me, this foolish destiny!
바보- fool; 같은- like; 운명아- destiny; 욕해- insult

(Run)
Don't tell me bye bye
(Run)
You make me cry cry
(Run)
Love is a lie lie
Don't tell me, don't tell me
Don't tell me bye bye
Don't tell me bye bye

다 끝난 거라는데 난 멈출 수가 없네
Everybody say it is over but I can't stop this
다- all; 끝난- end; 거라는데- say
땀인지 눈물인지 나 더는 분간 못해 oh
I can't tell whether it is sweat or tears
땀(인지)- sweat(or); 눈물(인지)- tears(or); 분간- discrimination, analysis
내 발가벗은 사랑도 거친 태풍 바람도
My bare-love and tough typhoon and wind
발가벗은- naked; 거친- tough, rough; 태풍- typhoon; 바람- wind
나를 더 뛰게만 해 내 심장과 함께
Can only make me run more with my heart
뛰게- run; 심장(과)- heart(with); 함께- together

더 뛰게 해줘
Let me run more
나를 더 뛰게 해줘
Please let me run more

두 발에 상처만 가득해도
Even though my feet are full of scars
니 얼굴만 보면 웃는 나니까

I smile whenever I see you

다시 Run Run Run 난 멈출 수가 없어
Let's run run run again! I can't stop running
또 Run Run Run 난 어쩔 수가 없어
Let's run run run again! I can't help running
어차피 이것밖에 난 못해
Only thing I can do is run
너를 사랑하는 것 밖엔 못해
Only thing I can do is love you

다시 Run Run Run 넘어져도 괜찮아
Let's run run run again! It's ok to fall down
또 Run Run Run 좀 다쳐도 괜찮아
Let's run run run again! It's ok to be injured
가질 수 없다 해도 난 족해
I am happy enough even though I can't get you
바보 같은 운명아 나를 욕해
Curse me, this foolish destiny!

추억들이 마른 꽃잎처럼 산산이 부서져가
Memories are crumbling like dried flower leaves
추억들- memories; 마른- dry; 꽃잎~처럼- like; 산산이- piece by piece
부서져가- breaking apart, crumbling apart
내 손 끝에서 내 발 밑에서
On my fingertips and under my feet
끝(에서)- end(at); 밑에서- under
달려가는 네 등 뒤로
running behind my back
등- back; 뒤로- behind
마치 나비를 쫓듯 꿈 속을 헤매듯 너의 흔적을 따라가
Like chasing butterfly or wondering in dreams I follow your traces
마치- finally; 나비- butterfly; 쫓(듯)- (as if) chasing; 헤매- wonder
흔적- trace; 따라가- follow
길을 알려줘 날 좀 멈춰줘
Please guide me please stop me
길- street; 알려줘- show, guide
날 숨쉬게 해줘
Please let me breathe

숨쉬게- breath

다시 Run Run Run 난 멈출 수가 없어
Let's run run run again! I can't stop running
또 Run Run Run 난 어쩔 수가 없어
Let's run run run again! I can't help running
어차피 이것밖에 난 못해
Only thing I can do is run
너를 사랑하는 것 밖엔 못해
Only thing I can do is love you

다시 Run Run Run 넘어져도 괜찮아
Let's run run run again! It's ok to fall down
또 Run Run Run 좀 다쳐도 괜찮아
Let's run run run again! It's ok to be injured
가질 수 없다 해도 난 족해
I am happy enough even though I can't get you
바보 같은 운명아 나를 욕해
Curse me, this foolish destiny!

(Run)
Don't tell me bye bye
(Run)
You make me cry cry
(Run)
Love is a lie lie
Don't tell me, don't tell me
Don't tell me bye bye

# *War of Hormone*

## Lyrics/Translation/Notes

(누구 때문에?) 여자 때문에
(Because of who?) Because of girls
(누구 때문에?) 호르몬
(Because of what?) Hormones
(누구 때문에?)

존재해 줘서 (참) 감사해
Thank you for existing
존재해- existing; 참- very, much 감사해- thanks
전화 좀 해줘 내가 (함) 밥 살게
Please call me, I'll buy you food
전화- call, telephone; 함- ham; 밥- rice, food; 살게- buy
아 요즘 미친 미친 거 같아 기침 기침
I think I'm crazy these days
요즘- these days; 기침- cough
하게 만드는 여자들 옷차림
Girls wear things that make me cough cough,
하게- do; 만드는-making; 여자들- girls; 옷차림- clothes, wardrobes

다 비침 비침
see right through, see right through
(베리마취) 땡큐! 내 시력을 올려줘
(Very much) thank you! For improving my eye sight
시력- vision; 올려줘- raising, improving

(자연라식) 돈 들일 필요 없어
(Natural LASIK) Don't need to spend money on that
돈- money; 들일- spend
I'll be in panic I'll be a fan
And I'll be a man of you you you you babe

자꾸만 눈이 돌아가네 여자들의 배 (Yup)
My eyes keep turning to the girls (yup)
자꾸만- often; 눈- eyes; 돌아가네- turning; 배- tummy, stomach
여자들은 방정식 우리 남자들은 해 (Yup)
Girls are like an equation, us guys just do them (yup)
방정식- equation;

땀 삘삘 괜히 빌빌대게 돼 더 많이 좀 신어줘 하이힐힐
I keep sweating and wishing. Wear them more, your high heels
땀- sweat; 괜히- uselessly; 신어- wear; 하이힐- high heel

나도 열여덟 알 건 다 알아
I'm 18, I know what I need to know
열여덟- 18

여자가 세계 최고란 것 말이여
I know that girls are the best things in the world
세계- world; 최고- best; ~란- with, in; 말이여- in the end
Yes I'm a bad boy so i like bad girl
일루 와봐 baby 우린 잘 될 걸
Come here baby, we're gonna hit it off
일루- here; 와- come; 잘 될 걸- will become good

(Hello hello) (What!)
(Hello hello) (What!)
Tell me what you want right now
(Hello hello) (What!)
(Hello hello) (What!)
Imma give it to you girl right now
내 껀 아니라지만 넌 최고
Imma give it to you girl right now
You're not mine but you're the best

껀- thing; 아니라(지(0 만)- not(but); 최고- best
니 앞에서 배배 꼬이는 내 몸
My body twists and turns in front of you
앞에서- in front of; 배배- baby, baby; 꼬이는- twisting; 몸- body
네게 다가서고 싶지만 너무 심하게 아름다워
I want to approach you but you're seriously too beautiful
다가서고- approach; 싶(지만)- want(but), 심하게- seriously; 아름다워-
beautiful

여자는 최고의
Girls are the best
선물이야 선물이야
Present! Present!
진짜 내 소원은
Really my wish is
소원- wish
너뿐이야 너뿐이야
Only you, only you

난 너라면 I'm ok
If it's you, I'm ok
Oh 자제가 안돼 매일
Oh, I can't hold back every day
자제가- self control; 안돼- can't be; 매일- every day
앞태도 최고 뒤태도 최고
Your front is the best, your back is the best
앞태- front side; 뒤태- back side
머리부터 발끝까지 최고 최고
From your head to your toes, you're the best
머리(부터)- head(from); 발끝(까지)- toe(to)

La la la la la la la la la
앞태도 최고 뒤태도 최고
Your front is the best, your back is the best
La la la la la la la la la
머리부터 발끝까지 최고 최고
From your head to your toes, you're the best

La la la la la la la la la

앞태도 최고 뒤태도 최고
Your front is the best, your back is the best
La la la la la la la la la
걸음걸이 하나까지 최고 최고
Even your walk is the best
걸음걸- stride

어림 반푼어치 없지 한두 번씩
There's not even a trace of rough, one two times
어림- rough; 반푼어치- penny side
놀다 헤어질 여자들에겐 관심 없지
I don't care about girls I'll play with once and say goodbye
놀다- to play; 헤어질- to break up; 관심- regard, concern
근데 널 보며 배워 body 건축학개론
But I learn when I see you, Body 101
근데- but; 배워- learn; 건축학개론- architecture lesson
묵직하게 증가하는 나의 테스토스테론
My testosterone heavily shows up
묵직하게- heavily; 증가하는- increasing; 테스토스테론- testosterone
호르몬과의 싸움 이겨낸 다음
After winning a war of hormones
호르몬과의- hormones'; 싸움- fight; 이겨낸- won; 다음- next, after
연구해 너란 존재는
I'll do some research, your existence
연구해- research; 존재- existence
반칙이야 파울
is against the rules, a foul
반칙- unlawfulness; 파울- foul
미적 기준이 바다면
If the standard of beauty is in the ocean,
미적- beauty, aesthetic; 기준- standard; 바다- sea, ocean
넌 좀 심해 그 자체
you're the Seriously Sea 1
심해- serious; 그 자체- that self
국가 차원에서
At the national level,
국- country; 차원- dimension

관리해야 될 미형 문화재
your beautiful form should be regarded
관리해야- should regulate; 미형- beauty form; 문화재- cultural asset

그녀 머리 바디 허리 다리
Her hair, body, waist, legs,
말 못하는 범위까지
even her other unspeakable parts
말 못하는- unspeakable; 범위- part, range

관심 없단 말이 남자로선 많이 어이상실
Saying I don't care would be ridiculous as a guy
관심- concern; 남자로선- as a man; 많이- much; 어이상실- ridiculous

작은 제스쳐 하나에도 뻑이 가지
I lose it just at her tiniest gestures
작은- small; 제스쳐- gesture; 뻑이- horny; 가지- branch

Girl 니 유혹에 밤마다 지켜
Girl, your temptations I care of nightly
유혹- temptation; 지켜- take care of

내 컴퓨터 자리
from my computer every night
자리- place

그녀를 위한 lady first
For her, it's lady first
위한- for

여잔 차가운 빙산? Let it go
Girls are like cold glaciers? Let it go
차가운- cold; 빙산- glacier

날 미치게 하는 female 날 자극하지 매일
A female that drives me crazy, provoking me every day
자극하지- provoke

오늘도 호르몬과의 싸움 후
After fighting my hormones again today,
후- after

내 여드름을 째
I'll pop my pimple
여드름- pimple; 째- pop

(Hello hello) (What!)
(Hello hello) (What!)

Tell me what you want right now
(Hello hello) (What!)
(Hello hello) (what!)
Imma give it to you girl right now
내 껀 아니라지만 넌 최고
You're not mine but you're the best
니 앞에서 배배 꼬이는 내 몸
My body twists and turns in front of you
네게 다가서고 싶지만 너무 심하게 아름다워
I want to approach you but you're seriously too beautiful

여자는 최고의
Girls are the best
선물이야 선물이야
Present! Present!
진짜 내 소원은
My real wish is
너뿐이야 너뿐이야
Only you, only you

난 너라면 I'm ok
If it's you, I'm ok
Oh 자제가 안돼 매일
Oh, I can't hold back every day
앞태도 최고 뒤태도 최고
Your front is the best, your back is the best
머리부터 발끝까지 최고 최고
From your head to your toes, you're the best

(누구 때문에?) 여자 때문에
(Because of who?) Because of girls
(누구 때문에?) 호르몬 때문에
(Because of what?) Because of hormones
(누구 때문에?) 남자기 때문에
(Because of what?) Because I'm a guy
(남자기 때문에?) 여자 때문에
(Because I'm a guy?) Because you're a girl
(누구 때문에?) 여자 때문에
(Because of who?) Because of girls
(누구 때문에?) 호르몬 때문에
(Because of what?) Because of hormones

(누구 때문에?) 남자기 때문에
(Because of what?) Because I'm a guy
(남자기 때문에?) 여자 때문에
(Because I'm a guy?) Because you're a girl

여자는 최고의
Girls are the best
선물이야 선물이야
Present! Present!
진짜 내 소원은
My real wish is
너뿐이야 너뿐이야
Only you, only you

난 너라면 I'm ok
If it's you, I'm ok
Oh 자제가 안돼 매일
Oh, I can't hold back every day
앞 태도 최고 뒤 태도 최고
Your front is the best, your back is the best
머리부터 발끝까지 최고 최고
From your head to your toes, you're the best

La la la la la la la la la
앞 태도 최고 뒤 태도 최고
Your front is the best, your back is the best
La la la la la la la la la
머리부터 발끝까지 최고 최고
From your head to your toes, you're the best

La la la la la la la la la
앞 태도 최고 뒤 태도 최고
Your front is the best, your back is the best
La la la la la la la la la
걸음걸이 하나까지 최고 최고
Even your walk is the best

# *No More Dream*

## Lyrics/Translation/Notes

얌마 니 꿈은 뭐니
Hey you, what's your dream?
얌마- you!; 뭐- what; ~니- (question tag)
얌마 니 꿈은 뭐니
Hey you, what's your dream?
얌마 니 꿈은 뭐니
Hey you, what's your dream?
니 꿈은 겨우 그거니
Is your dream only that?
겨우- only

I wanna big house, big cars & big rings
But 사실은 I dun have any big dreams
But actually, I don't have any big dreams
하하 난 참 편하게 살어
Haha, I live quite comfortably
참- very, quite; 편하게- comfortably; 살어- live
꿈 따위 안 꿔도 아무도 뭐라 안 하잖어
Even if I don't dream, no one says anything
꿔다- to dream; 아무도- no one

전부 다다다 똑가같이
Everyone, all all all, the same
나처럼 생각하고 있어
the same thinking as me
전부- all; 똑가같이- together, the same
새까까까맣게 까먹은
꿈 많던 어린 시절
I completely forgot about my childhood
대학은 걱정 마
Don't worry about college,
대학- college; 걱정- worry; 마- don't
멀리라도 갈 거니까
I had far places to go
멀리라도- far; 갈 거니까- because I'll go
알았어 엄마 지금 독서실 간다니까
Ok mom, I'm going to the library right now
알았어- I know; 독서실- library

니가 꿈꿔온 니 모습이 뭐여
What is the you that you've dreamed of?
꿈꿔온- dream; 모습이- appearance
지금 니 거울 속엔 누가 보여, I gotta say
Who do you see in the mirror? I gotta say
거울- mirror
너의 길을 가라고
Go on your path
길- path, road
단 하루를 살아도
Even if you live for only a day
단- only; 하루- day
뭐라도 하라고
Do something
나약함은 담아둬
Put away your weakness
나약함- weakness; 담아둬- put down, put away

왜 말 못하고 있어?
Why can't you saying anything?

72

왜- why; 말- speech; ~하고 있어- (~ing- continuous form)

공부는 하기 싫다면서 학교 때려 치기는 겁나지?

You don't wanna study but you're scared to quit school?

싫다(면서)- dislike(as); 학교- school; 때려- hit; 치기는- quitting

이거 봐 등교할 준비하네 벌써

See, you're already getting ready for school.

등교- school registration; 준비하네- get ready; 벌써- already

철 좀 들어 제발 좀, 너 입만 살아가지고

Please grow up, you're all talk dude,

철- season, iron; 들어- get, hold; 제발- please; 입- mouth

임마 유리멘탈 boy

you have a glass mentality, boy

유리-glass; 멘탈- mental

(Stop!) 자신에게 물어봐 언제 니가 열심히 노력했냐고

(Stop) Ask yourself if you've ever worked hard for anything

자신(에게)- self(to); 물어봐- ask; 열심히- strenuously; 노력- try; ~냐고- asking


얌마 니 꿈은 뭐니

Hey you, what's your dream?

얌마 니 꿈은 뭐니

Hey you, what's your dream?

얌마 니 꿈은 뭐니

Hey you, what's your dream?

니 꿈은 겨우 그거니

Is that all your dream is?


거짓말이야 you such a liar

That's a lie, you such a liar

See me see me ya 넌 위선자야

왜 자꾸 딴 길을 가래 야 너나 잘해

See me, see me, ya you're a hypocrite

Why're you telling to go a different path? Take care of yourself

위선자- hypocrite; 자꾸- often; 딴- different

제발 강요하진 말아줘

Please don't force me

(La la la la la)

니 꿈이 뭐니 니 꿈이 뭐니 뭐니

What's your dream, what's your dream?

(La la la la la)

73

고작 이거니 고작 이거니 거니
Is that it? Is that it?

지겨운 same day, 반복되는 매일에
Sick of the same day, the repeating days
지겨운- boring; 반복되는- repeating

어른들과 부모님은
Grown-ups and my parents
어른들- adults; 부모님- parents

틀에 박힌 꿈을 주입해
keep instilling confined dreams to me
틀- frame; 박힌- confined; 주입해- insert

장래희망 넘버원.. 공무원?
Number one future career is a government worker?
장래- future; 희망- ambition; 넘버원- number one; 공무원- government
employee

강요된 꿈은 아냐, 9 회말 구원투수
It's not a forced dream, a ninth inning relief pitcher
강요된- forced; 회말- nineth inning; 구원- relief; 투수- pitcher

시간낭비인 야자에 돌직구를 날려
Throw a fast ball at the waste of time that is night study sessions
시간낭비인- waste of time; 야자- nighttime; 돌직구- fast ball

지옥 같은 사회에 반항해
Rebel against the hellish society,
지옥- hell; 같은- like; 사회- society; 반항- rebel against

특별사면
special pardon

자신에게 물어봐 니 꿈의 profile 억압만 받던 인생
Ask yourself about your dream profile; a life only suppressed
억압만- suppression; 받던- received; 인생- life

니 삶의 주어가 되어봐
Become the main subject of your life
주어가- subject

니가 꿈꿔온 니 모습이 뭐여
What is the you that you've dreamed of?

지금 니 거울 속엔 누가 보여, I gotta say
Who do you see in the mirror? I gotta say

너의 길을 가라고
Go on your path
단 하루를 살아도
Even if you live for a day
뭐라도 하라고 나약함은 담아둬
Do something. Put away your weakness

얌마 니 꿈은 뭐니
Hey you, what's your dream?
얌마 니 꿈은 뭐니
Hey you, what's your dream?
얌마 니 꿈은 뭐니
Hey you, what's your dream?
니 꿈은 겨우 그거니
Is that all your dream is?

거짓말이야 you such a liar
That's a lie, you such a liar
See me see me ya 넌 위선자야
See me, see me, ya you're a hypocrite.
왜 자꾸 딴 길을 가래 야 너나 잘해
Why're you telling to go a different path? Take care of yourself
제발 강요하진 말아줘
Please don't force me
(La la la la la)
니 꿈이 뭐니 니 꿈이 뭐니 뭐니
What's your dream, what's your dream?
(La la la la la)
고작 이거니 고작 이거니 거니
Is that it? Is that it?

살아가는 법을 몰라
Don't know how to live
날아가는 법을 몰라
Don't know how to fly
결정하는 법을 몰라
Don't know how to decide
이젠 꿈꾸는 법도 몰라
Don't know how to dream now
눈을 눈을 눈을 떠라 다 이제
Open your eyes now

춤을 춤을 춤을 춰봐 자 다시
Dance a dance now
꿈을 꿈을 꿈을 꿔봐 다
Dream a dream now
너 꾸물대지마 우물쭈물 대지마 wussup!
Stop hesitating, stop being indecisive, wussup!
꾸물대지마- don't fool around; 우물쭈물 대지마- don't be indecisive

거짓말이야 you such a liar
That's a lie, you such a liar
거짓말- a lie
See me see me ya 넌 위선자야
See me, see me, ya you're a hypocrite
왜 자꾸 딴 길을 가래 야 너나 잘해
Why're you telling to go a different path? Take care of yourself
제발 강요하진 말아줘
Please don't force me
(La la la la la)
니 꿈이 뭐니 니 꿈이 뭐니 뭐니
What's your dream, what's your dream?
(La la la la la)
고작 이거니 고작 이거니 거니
Is that it? Is that it?

To all the youngsters without dreams.

# *Dope*

## Lyrics/Translation/Notes

어서 와 방탄은 처음이지?
Welcome, first time with BTS?
어서 와- Welcome; 처음이(지)- first time(question tag)

Ayo ladies & gentleman
준비가 됐다면 부를게 yeah!
If you're ready, I'll start, yeah!
딴 녀석들과는 다르게
Differently from other guys
딴- other; 녀석들(과)- guys(with); 다르게- different
내 스타일로 내 내 내 내 스타일로 에오!
With my style, with my style, ayo!

밤새 일했지 everyday
I worked all night, every day
니가 클럽에서 놀 때 yeah
While you were playing in the club
자 놀라지 말고 들어 매일
Don't be surprised and listen every day
놀라지- surprised; 클럽- club
I got a feel, I got a feel
난 좀 쩔어!
I'm kinda sick!
쩔어- sick

아 쩔어 쩔어 쩔어 우리 연습실 땀내봐 쩌렁 쩌렁 쩌렁한
Sick sick sick, the smell of sweat in our studio
연습실- practice room

내 춤이 답해
my ringing dance moves answer

모두 비실이 찌질이 찡찡이 띨띨이들
All of you are so weak, such losers, crybabies and idiots

나랑은 상관이 없어
Has nothing to do with me
나랑- with me; 상관- concern

cuz 난 희망이 쩔어 haha
cuz I'm sick with hope haha

Ok 우린 머리부터 발끝까지 전부 다 쩌 쩔어
OK, we're sick from our head to our toes

하루의 절반을 작업에 쩌 쩔어
We're sick with work for half our days
절반- half day; 작업- job, operation

작업실에 쩔어 살어 청춘은 썩어가도
We live sickly in our studios, our youths may rot away
작업실- office, studio; 청춘- youth; 썩어- rot

덕분에 모로 가도 달리는 성공가도
But thanks to that, we're running to success
덕분에- thanks; 모로- side; 달리는- running; 성공-success

소녀들아 더 크게 소리질러 쩌 쩌렁
Girls, scream louder, let it ring
소녀들- girls; 크게- big, loud; 쩌렁- ring

밤새 일했지 everyday
I worked all night, every day
일했지- worked

니가 클럽에서 놀 때 yeah
While you were playing in the club
때- when, while

딴 녀석들과는 다르게
Differently from other guys
I don't wanna say yes
I don't wanna say yes

소리쳐봐 all right
Make some noise, all right
몸이 타버리도록 all night (all night)
Till your body burns up, all night (all night)
타버리(도록)- (like) burning up
Cause we got fire (fire!)
Higher (higher!)
I gotta make it, I gotta make it
쩔어!
I gotta make it, I gotta make it
It's sick!

거부는 거부해
Reject rejection
난 원래 너무해
I was always too much
모두 다 따라 해
쩔어
Everyone follow me
It's sick

거부는 거부해
Reject rejection
전부 나의 노예
You are all my slaves
노예- slaves
모두 다 따라 해
Everyone follow me
쩔어
It's sick

3 포세대? 5 포세대?
Third generation? Fifth generation?
세대- generation
그럼 난 육포가 좋으니까 6 포세대
Well I like beef jerky so it's 6th generation
언론과 어른들은 의지가 없다며
The media and adults say we don't have willpower,
언론- media; 어른- adult; 의지- will
우릴 싹 주식처럼 매도해

79

condemning us like stocks
주식- stocks; 매도해- condemn

왜 해보기도 전에 죽여 걔넨 enemy enemy enemy
Why are they killing us before we can even try, enemy enemy enemy
해보(기도)- (even) attempt; 전에- before

왜 벌써부터 고개를 숙여 받아 energy energy energy
Why are you hanging your head and accepting it already? energy energy energy
고개- head; 숙여- hang; 받아- receive

절대 마 포기 you know you not lonely
Don't ever give up, you know you not lonely
절대- absolutely; 포기- quit

너와 내 새벽은 낮보다 예뻐
Our dawn is prettier than the day
새벽- dawn; 낮- day; 예뻐- pretty
So can I get a little bit of hope? (yeah)
잠든 청춘을 깨워 go
Wake your sleeping youth, go
깨워- wake

밤새 일했지 everyday
I worked all night, every day
니가 클럽에서 놀 때 yeah
While you were playing in the club
딴 녀석들과는 다르게
Differently from other guys
I don't wanna say yes
I don't wanna say yes

소리쳐봐 all right
Make some noise, all right
몸이 타버리도록 all night (all night)
Till your body burns up, all night (all night)
Cause we got fire (fire!)
Cause we got fire (fire!)
Higher (higher!)
I gotta make it, I gotta make it
쩔어!
I gotta make it, I gotta make it
It's sick!

거부는 거부해
Reject rejection
난 원래 너무해
I was always too much
모두 다 따라 해
쩔어
Everyone follow me
It's sick

거부는 거부해
Reject rejection
전부 나의 노예
You are all my slaves
모두 다 따라 해
쩔어
Everyone follow me
It's sick

이런 게 방탄 스타일
This is the Bangtan style
거짓말 wack 들과는 달라
Different from the lying wack jobs
거짓말- a lie; 달라- different
매일이 hustle life
Every day is about the hustle life
I gotta make it fire baby

이런 게 방탄 스타일
This is the Bangtan style
거짓말 wack 들과는 달라
Different from the lying wack jobs
매일이 hustle life
Every day is about the hustle life
I gotta make it, I gotta make it
난 좀 쩔어!
I gotta make it, I gotta make it
I'm kinda sick!

Say what!
Say wo~ wo~
Say what!

쩔어

# *Young Forever*

## Lyrics/Translation/Notes

막이 내리고 나는 숨이 차
The curtain falls and I'm out of breath
막- curtain, block; 내리(고)- come down(and); 차- car, vehicle
복잡해진 마음, 숨을 내쉰다
I get mixed feelings as I breathe out
복잡해진- become complicated; 마음- mind; 내쉰다- breathe out
오늘 뭐 실수는 없었었나
Did I make any mistakes today
오늘- today; 뭐- what; 실수- mistake
관객들의 표정은 어땠던가
How did the audience seem
관객들- audience; 표정- appearance; 어땠던가- how?
그래도 행복해 난 이런 내가 돼서
I'm happy with who I've become
그래도- regardless of that; 행복해- be happy; 이런- like this; 돼서-
became
누군가를 소리 지르게 만들 수가 있어서
That I can make someone scream with joy
누군가- whoever; 소리-noise, sound; 지르게 - shout; 만들 수가 있어서- can
make
채 가시지 않은 여운들을 품에 안고
Full of the lingering impressions I don't let go
채 가시지 않은 여운들을 품에 안고

채- my; 가시지- going; 여운들- lingering images; 품에 안고- hold to breast

아직도 더운 텅 빈 무대에 섰을 때
I still stand on the hot, empty stage
더운- hot; 텅- all; 빈- emptly; 무대- stage; 섰다- to stand


더운 텅 빈 무대에 섰을 때
I still stand on the hot, empty stage
괜한 공허함에 난 겁을 내
And suddenly I feel so afraid of the void
괜한- suddenly; 공허함- void; 겁을 내- give the fear

복잡한 감정 속에서 삶의 사선 위에서
Inside the complex emotions, for my lifeline
감정- emotion, feeling; 삶- life; 사선- lifeline; 위에서- for

괜시리 난 더 무딘 척을 해
I pretend to be careless
괜시리- okay condition; 무딘- careless; 척- pretending

괜시리 난 더 무딘 척을 해
I pretend to be careless
처음도 아닌데 익숙해질 법한데
This isn't the first time, I better get used to it
처음- first; 익숙해질- will get used to; 법- method, rule

숨기려 해도 그게 안돼
I try to hide it, but I can't
숨기(려)- (in order to) hide; 안돼- not making it

텅 빈 무대가 식어갈 때쯤
Until the emptiness of the stage withers away
식어갈- withers

빈 객석을 뒤로하네
I leave the empty seats behind
객석- seats; 뒤(로)- behind(around)


지금 날 위로하네 완벽한 세상은
I comfort myself, a perfect world
위로하다- to comfort; 완벽한- perfect; 세상- world

없다고 자신에게 말해 난
isn't, I tell myself.
없(다고)0- don't have(say); 자신- myself; ~에게- to

점점 날 비워가네 언제까지 내 것일
Bit by bit I empty all, until forever I can't make
점점- slowly, little by little; 비워가네- let go, empty away

순 없어 큰 박수갈채가
the great cheering applause mine
큰- big; 박수- applause; 갈채가- cheering

이런 내게 말을 해, 뻔뻔히
Here I tell myself, shamelessly
뻔뻔히- shamelessly

니 목소릴 높여 더 멀리
Raise your voice higher, farther
니- your; 목소리- voice; 높- high; 멀리- far

영원한 관객은 없대도
Even if the attention isn't forever,
영원한- forever; 관객- audience

난 노래할 거야
I'll keep singing
거야- (future imperative)

오늘의 나로 영원하고파
Today's eternity for me
오늘의 나로 영원하고파
Today's eternity for me
영원히 소년이고 싶어 난 Aah
I want to stay young forever
소년- boy, youth

Forever we are young
나리는 꽃잎 비 사이로
Between the flying petals and the rain
나리는- flying, blown; 꽃잎- petals; 비- rain; 사이로- between
나리는 꽃잎 비 사이로
Between the flying petals and the rain
헤매어 달리는 이 미로
I run, so lost in this maze
헤매어- lost, confused; 미로- maze
Forever we are young
넘어져 다치고 아파도
Even when I fall and hurt myself
넘어져- fallen; 다치다- to injure; 아파- hurt

85

끝없이 달리네 꿈을 향해
I keep running toward my dream
끝없이- endlessly; 향해- toward

Forever ever ever ever
(꿈, 희망, 전진, 전진)
(dreams, hopes, forward, forward)
Forever ever ever we are young

Forever ever ever ever
(꿈, 희망, 전진, 전진)
(dreams, hopes, forward, forward)
Forever ever ever we are young

Forever we are young
나리는 꽃잎 비 사이로
Between the flying petals and the rain
헤매어 달리는 이 미로
I run, so lost in this maze
Forever we are young
넘어져 다치고 아파도
Even when I fall and hurt myself
끝없이 달리네 꿈을 향해
I keep running toward my dream

Forever we are young
나리는 꽃잎 비 사이로
Between the flying petals and the rain
헤매어 달리네 이 미로
I run, so lost in this maze
Forever we are young
넘어져 다치고 아파도
Even when I fall and hurt myself
끝없이 달리네 꿈을 향해
I keep running toward my dream

# *We Are Bulletproof*

## Lyrics/Translation/Notes

(What) 이리 내놔(What) Give it to me

(What) 긴장해 다(What) Be nervous

(What) 끝판대장(What) The one to end it all
(What) We are bulletproof
We are bulletproof
Bulletproof

이름은 Jung Kook, 스케일은 전국
The name is Jung Kook, my scale is nationwide
이름- name; 전국- nationwide; 전- much, all; 국- country, nation
학교 대신 연습실에서 밤새
Instead of school, all night in the practice room
학교- school; 대신- instead; 연습-practice; 실- room
춤을 추고 노래 불렀네
I danced and sang.
춤- dance; 추고- danced; 노래- song; 불렀네- sang
너희가 놀 때, 난 꿈을
When you guys partied, my dreams
너희가- you all; 놀- play; 때- when
집도하며 잠을 참아가며
I kept and let go sleep.

집도하(며)- kept(and); 잠- sleep; 참아가며- patiently go

매일 밤새 볼펜을 잡네

I spent all night holding a pen,

매일- everyday; 밤새- all night; 볼펜- ballpen; 잡네- hold

아침 해가 뜬 뒤에 나 눈을 감네

closing my eyes only after the morning sun rises

아침- morning; 해가- sun; 뜬- opened, floated; 뒤에- after; 눈을 감네- closed eyes.

이중잣대와 수많은 반대 속에서

double standards and many oppositions

이중잣대와- double standards; 잣대- standards; 수많은- many; 반대- opposing

깨부숴버린 나의 한계

My limit was broken in the

깨부숴버린- broken and wasted; 한계- limit

그에 반해 재수 좋게 회사에 컨택된 속칭

But I got lucky; a new beginning with an agency's contact

그에 반해- to the contrary; 재수- luck, fortune; 회사- company;

컨택- contact; 된- become; 속칭- New Year

노래 못 해 랩퍼를 당한

You can't sing; hurting rappers

랩퍼- rapper; 당한- insulted, assaulted

너희에게 랩퍼라는 타이틀은 사치

The rapper title is an extravagance for you

타이틀- title; 사치- luxury


Everywhere I go, everything I do

나 보여줄게 칼을 갈아왔던 만큼

I will show you, as much as I sharpened my sword

보여줄게- show; 칼- knife, sword; 갈아왔던- sharpened up

날 무시하던 많은 사람들 이젠

To all the people who looked down on me

날(나를); 무시하던- ignoring


Oh! 나만치 해봤다면 돌을 던져

Oh! If you've done as much as me, throw a stone

만치- as far as; 해봤다면- if attempted; 돌- stone; 던져- throw

Oh! 나만치 해봤다면 돌을 던져

Oh! If you've done as much as me, throw a stone

We go hard 우린 겁이 없어
We go hard, we have no fear
우린- we; 겁- fear
(Click click, bang bang) we juss sing it like
(Click click, bang bang) we juss sing it like
Oh! 나만치 해봤다면 돌을 던져 Oh!
Oh! If you've done as much as me, throw a stone
We go hard 우린 겁이 없어
We go hard, we have no fear

(What) 이리 내놔(What) Give it to me
(What) 긴장해 다(What) Be nervous
(What) 끝판대장(What) The one to end it all
(What) We are bulletproof
We are bulletproof
Bulletproof

Look at my profile, 아직 아무것도 없지
Look at my profile, there's nothing there yet
아직- still; 아무것도- nothing
Still 연습생 and 랩퍼맨,
Still a trainee and rapper man,
yeah I do know that's nuthin
고민도 했지만 이제 필요 없어졌지
I stressed a lot but now I don't need anything
고민- concern, worry; ~지만- but; 필요- need; 없어졌지- disappeared
넌 아직도 아마추어,
You're still an amateur,
아직도- still; 아마추어- amateur
난 메이저, 쭉 그렇게 썩길
I'm in the majors, you on the rotten path
메이저- major; 쭉- straight; 그렇게- like that; 썩길- rotting way
랩몬스터, 말처럼 괴물같이
Rap Monster, like words of a monster
~처럼- as, like 괴물- monster; ~같이- like
무슨 비트든 간에 난 싹 집어삼켜
I can eat up any kind of beat like a monster
무슨- whatever; 간- liver; 싹- completely; 집어삼켜- eat up

충실한 이름값 얘들아 이리와
I'm loyal to my name, guys come here
충실한- loyal, faithful; 이름-name; 얘들아- guys; 이리와- come

충실한 이름값 얘들아 이리와
I'm loyal to my name, guys come here,
미리 봐 한낱 아이돌의 반전
take a preview, I put a twist to being an idol
미리- in advance; 봐- see; 한낱- just, only; 반전- reversal, twist

미리 봐 한낱 아이돌의 반전
하하 힙부심뿐인 형들은
Haha, hyungs who only had hip-hop pride
힙부심- hip hop pride; 뿐- only; 인- person; 형들은- hyungs, brothers

불가능하다 했지 but
told me it'd be impossible but
불가능하다- to be impossible

똑똑히 봐 이걸 impossible 에 마침표
Look close, I place a period after impossible
똑똑히- clearly, carefully; 마침- end; 표- sign

찍어 I'm possible 자 이제 됐니 boy
Impress it, I'm possible, now are we all set, boy?
찍어- impress, take in; 이제 됐니- all right, now?; 니- (question tag)

Everywhere I go, everything I do
나 보여줄게 칼을 갈아왔던 만큼
I will show you, as much as I sharpened my sword
날 무시하던 많은 사람들 이젠
To all the people who looked down on me
(Oh oh oh oh oh oh) hey shout it out

Oh! 나만치 해봤다면 돌을 던져 Oh! Throw a stone at me if you've done as much as I did
We go hard 우린 겁이 없어 We go hard, we have no fear

(Click click, bang bang) We juss sing it like
(Click click, bang bang) We juss sing it like
Oh! 나만치 해봤다면 돌을 던져 Oh! Throw a stone at me if you've done as much as I did
We go hard 우린 겁이 없어 We go hard, we have no fear
(Click click, bang bang) We juss sing it like
(Click click, bang bang) We juss sing it like

(What) 이리 내놔(What) Give it to me

(What) 긴장해 다(What) Be nervous

(What) 끝판대장(What) The one to end it all

(What) We are bulletproof
We are bulletproof
Bulletproof

Bulletproof.

# *Cypher Pt. 3*

## Lyrics/Translation/Notes

<u>니가 무엇을 하든 I will kill for</u>
Whatever you do, I will kill for
무엇- whatever
<u>내가 무엇을 하든 I'll be real for</u>
Whatever I do, I'll be real for
똑바로 봐
Look carefully,
똑바로- straight, carefully
<u>이게 바로 니가 바 바란 beast mode</u>
this is what you wanted, the beast mode
바로- just, exactly; 바란- hoped
<u>남자는 담배,</u>
When men smoke;
담배- cigarettes
<u>여자는 바람 필 때</u>
girls are cheating
<u>바람- wind; 바람 필 때- cheating (colloquial)</u>
<u>I smoke beat this a beat smoke</u>

Who the man told you crazy
Who the fella told you crazy
I'm better than ya lazy

키보드로 힙합 하는 놈들보다
The bastards who do hiphop with keyboards
키보드- keyboard

백 배는 열심히 살지
I work a hundred times harder than
백- hundred; 배는- hundred; 열심히- hard, with effort

랩=만만한 genre,
Rap is an easy genre to them,
too many generals

어중이떠중이들아 다 갖춰라 매너를
You anyones and everyones, all have some manners
어중이떠중이들아- anyone and everyone

무슨 벌스 하나도 제대로 못 끌어가는
Bastards who can't even give a single verse properly
벌스- verse; 제대로- properly; 끌어가는- drawing, pulling

놈들이 랩이나 음악을 논하려 하니들
They try to discuss rap and music
음악- music; 논하려- 하니들

그래서 여기는 지금도 똑같이
That's why everyone raps
그래서- so; 똑같이- same

전부 다 이렇게 랩을 하지
completely the same way here
전부- completely

세 글자 아니면 두 글자씩밖에
If not three words only two at a time
글자-word; 씩- each

못 말해 다 중환자지
like some hospital patient
중- in, during; 환자- patient

Motherfather 실어증 환자들,
Motherfather verbal aphasia patients
실어증- aphasia

전부 사짜들
They're all fakes,
사짜- fake, dummy
back yourself and look at the mirror
가져올라면
If you wanna bring some,
독창적으로 좀 해봐 뭐 suckas
bring it originally suckas,
독창적으로- ingeniously

성의들이 zero
you have zero sincerity
성의들- saints
I go by the name of monster
Welcome to the monster plaza
This a cypher im a rider
imma ride it like a biker
Oh 쉿 거꾸로 돌려봐 beat
Oh shit turn the beat backwards
거꾸로- backwards; 돌려- turn

넌 하수구 난 구수하지
You're like a sewer and I'm savory 1
하수구- drain; 구수- elegant, charming

실력이 파업중인 애들이
Kids whose skills have gone on strike
실력- skill; 파업중인- on strike

내 뒤에서 시위는 겁나 하지
The protesters behind my back fear
뒤에서- behind; 시위는- protester 겁나 하지
Man what you afraid of
난 비트 위에서 당당해
I'm confident when I'm on the beat
당당해- be confident

넌 거진 다
You all be beggars
거지- beggar

주머니와 없는 실력까지가난해
Having no skills in bank so poor
주머니- pocket

I don't need GIVENCHY, cuz im a star
I don't need HUGO, already a boss
난 아냐 부처, but im a butcher
I'm not Buddha but I'm a butcher,
부처- Buddha

니 살을 깎아버려 like a
I'll cut away your skin like a
살- skin; 깎아- cut


바꿔라 니 iphone,
Change your iPhone;
you dont need your airplane mode
난 로밍 요금만 몇십 돈,
My roaming charges are hundreds
로밍- roaming; 요금- bill; ~만- just, only
and you know I can take it more
돈 벌어라 돌로, 팔어 돌이나 돌팔이들
Make money from rocks, sell rocks, you rock cobblers
벌어라- make money; 돌로- from rocks, 팔어- sell; 돌팔이들- rock
sellers
San paulo to Stockholm,
니넨 평생 못 앉을 자리들
seats that you all can never sit on in your lifetime
I sit
평생- life, lifetime; 자리들- seats, places

Hater 들은 많지
So many haters
But no problem, I kill
날 묻기 위해 내 커리어에다 파대는 삽질
They try to chip away my career to bury me

But I don't care
You can't control my 쉿
You can't control my shit
불신을 참아낸 닌자가 돼 다시 돌아왔지
I became a ninja who overcame disbelief and returned

이네 번째 앨범 정규의 관점 Cypher
The official standpoint of this fourth album is Cypher
이 트랙이 나오면 Hater 들 완전 암전
When this track comes out, haters will fall silent
불법인 이 씬에 이 곡은 합법, 함정
In this illegal scene, this track is the law
다 빠지겠지
Everyone will fall into the rap,
매일 다들 Hang hang over bang
every day, they hang hang over bang
터져 나와 Swag,
My swag explodes,
어딜 가든 직진
wherever I go, I'll go forward
또 어딜 가든 있지 모든 힙찌질이 힙찔
Wherever I go, there are hip-hop losers
비례적인 위치
I'm too busy for them
날 욕하기엔 Busy
to compare me and talk smack about me
But 난 입질 왔담 삐끼
But I'm getting a bite,
모든 언니 s call me 삐삐
all the touting girls call me Pippi

누가 날 보고 욕하고 그래
Who is talking smack about me?
니 상황이나 보고서 오라고 그래
Tell them to look at their own situation before doing that
난 남부러울 게 없어 다 보라고 그래

I have nothing to be jealous of, tell them to look at me
Oh 난 비트 비트 위
Oh I'm on the beat,
wiggle wiggling jingle jingling
뒹굴 뒹굴지, 비글 비글짓
Rolling around, beagle beagling
또 이글이글 힘,
With burning power,
지금 지금 링 위를 위를 지배를 하는 신
I'm the god who controls this ring,
이름 오를 킹
an ascending king

이건 맛보기일 뿐 아직은 간식
This is just a taste, it's just the appetizer
내 랩은 곧 니 배를 채우는 한식
My rap is like the Korean meal that fills your stomach
그래 내 나라 한국
Yeah, I'm from Korea,
어설픈 영어 지껄이는 랩 만식이들 다 봐라
so all you bastards who try to rap in English
지금 누가 니 위에 있는지 What
Look and see who's on top of you right now, what

Hater 들은 많지
So many haters
But no problem, I kill
날 묻기 위해 내 커리어에다 파대는 삽질
They try to chip away my career to bury me
묻기 위해- in order to bury; 삽질- spade

But I don't care
You can't control my 쉿
불신을 참아낸 닌자가 돼 다시 돌아왔지
I became a ninja who overcame disbelief and returned
불신- doubt, disbelief; 참아낸- overcame; 돼- became; 돌아왔지-
returned

SUGA a.k.a Agust D 두 번째 이름
SUGA a.k.a Agust D is my second name
길거리를 걸어 다니면 수군대 내 이름
When I'm walking on the street, people whisper my name
길거리- street; 걸어- walk; 다니다- go about; 수군거리다- to whisper
대구에서부터 압구정까지 깔아 놓은 내 비트
My beat spreads from Daegu to Apgujung
깔아- spread; 놓은- placed
전 세계 사방 곳곳 살아 숨쉬는 내 음악들의 생기
The life of my music lives and breathes all over the world
사방- living place, 생기- live
나는 비트란 작두를 타는
Riding the haycutter that is my beat,
작두- haycutter; 타는- riding
애기 무당, that's me
I'm a baby shaman, that's me
TV 속에 비치는 모습 반은
Did you know that half the things
반은- half
카게무샤인 건 아니
you see on TV are Kagemusha?
너의 세치 혀로 객기 부려봤자
You can try to make rash sounds with your bird tongue
세- bird; 혀- tongue; 객기- rash, drunken rashness
그건 rapping 호객 행위
That rapping is street selling
호객 행위- street touting

놈팽이들의 뺑끼를 향해 때리는
Hitting all the bums balls that play around
뺑끼- balls; 향해- be in the direction; 때리는- hitting
묵직한 내 패왕랩의 패기
The fighting spirit of my heavy king-like rap
묵직한- heavy weight; 왕-king; 패기- spirit

건방 떠는 rapper 듣보잡들을 잡아다
My flow job catches all the pretentious rappers
건방- arrogant; 떠는- vibrating

농락시켜버리는 내 flow job, 고작
Dispose of the games, my flow job only
농락- amusement; 고작- only, barely

그 따위 말로 날 극딜해봤자
You can try to get to me with those little words,
극딜해봤자- try and get

난 더 강해져 불가사의
but I'll just become stronger- it's a wonder
강해져- become stronger; 불가사- wonder, mystery

난 니들의 시기 질투를 먹고 자라는 불가사리
I'm a starfish that eats and grows on your time and envy
시기- time; 질투- jealousy; 불가사리- starfish

알다시피 내 목소린 좀 꼴림
As you know, my voice will turn you on
알다시피- as you know; 꼴림- hard on

남자든 여자든 랩으로 홍콩을
By rap I send boy or girl to mess up
보내는 유연한 내 혀놀림
Sending sinuous tongue play
보내는- sending; 유연한- lithe; 혀놀림- word play

이 먹이사슬 위
On this food chain,
먹이- food; 사슬- chain

난 항상 정상 위의 정상 최상위
I'm always on the top of the top
항상- always; 정상- normal, fair; 위의- top of; 최상위- very top

멈추지 않는 똘끼
My craziness won't stop
멈추지- stop; 똘끼- a tongue

누가 내 뒤에서 나를 엿맥이든
Even if someone betrays me from behind

누가- someone; 엿맥이든- betrayed, tied up

니들이 쳐놀 때 우린 세계일주

While you hit and play us, we're world-wide

쳐놀- play hit; 세계일주- around the world

나이를 허투루 쳐먹은 행님들

You hyungs who are getting older by the day

나이- age; 허투루- carelessly; 쳐먹은- eating

내 기준에서는 너도 애기 수준

In my standards, you all are like babies

기준- standard; 애기- baby; 수준- level

내가 뭐 wack 이든 내가 뭐 fake 이든

Whether you call me wack or fake

어쨌든 저쨌든 가요계 새 기준

Whatever my cut, I'm a new standard to kpop

어쨌든- whatever; 가요계- pop music; 새- new; 기준- standard

이 랩은 꼰대 귀때기에

This rap will cut through your ears

꼰- squirming, crossing; 귀때기에- to ear, to cut ear

쌔리는 폭풍 귀싸대기

A slap to your ears like a storm,

쌔리는 폭풍 귀싸대기

chop chop chop

Hater 들은 많지

So many haters

But no problem, I kill

날 묻기 위해 내 커리어에다 파대는 삽질

They try to chip away my career to bury me

But I don't care

You can't control my 쉣

You can't control my shit

불신을 참아낸 닌자가 돼 다시 돌아왔지

I became a ninja who overcame disbelief and returned

# Cypher Pt. 4

## Lyrics/Translation/Notes

"이름, 이름!" sorry bae"
Name, name!" sorry bae
"발음, 발음!" sorry bae
"Pronunciation, pronunciation!" sorry bae
"딕션, 딕션, 딕션!" sorry bae
"Diction, diction, diction!" sorry bae
"Oh, face not an idol.." sorry bae
"Oh, face not an idol.." sorry bae

숨쉬고 있어서 I'm sorry bae
I'm sorry bae because I'm breathing
너무 건강해서 I'm sorry bae
I'm sorry bae because I'm so healthy
방송합니다 I'm sorry bae
I'm sorry bae I'm broadcasting
Errthing errthing errthing
Errthing errthing errthing
Sorry bae Sorry bae
지금 내가 내는 소리 bae
The sound I'm making right now, bae
내는- giving

누군가에겐 개소리 bae
Is all dog noise to someone, bae
~에겐- to; 개- dog; 소리

까는 패턴 좀 바꾸지 bae
You should change your bashing pattern, bae
까는- bashing; 바꾸지- change

지루해질라캐 boring bae
It'll start to get boring, boring bae
지루하다- to bore

이젠 니가 안 미워
I don't dislike you anymore
안 미워- don't dislike

이젠 니가 안 미워 sorry bae
I don't dislike you anymore, sorry bae

북이 돼줄게 걍 쎄게 치고 말어
I'll be the drum, just hit me hard
북- drum; 돼줄게- become; 쎄게- will all might

그래 해보자 사물놀이 bae
Yes, try samulnoli, bae
사물놀이- (a kind of Korean traditional music)

난 괴물, 너무 길어 꼬리 bae
I'm a monster, my tail is too long, bae
괴물- monster; 너무- too, very; 길어- long; 꼬리- tail

어차피 넌 날 쏘지 bae
You'll shoot me anyway, bae
어차피- anyway; 쏘지- shoot

그럴 바엔 편해 동물원이 bae
In that case, a zoo would be more comfortable, bae
바- fate; 편해- be comfortable; 동물원- zoo

너도 원하잖아 씹을거리 bae
You want it too, something to chew on, bae
원하다- to want; 씹다- to chew

니가 날 싫어해도 you know me
Even if you don't like me, you know me

니가 날 싫어해도 you know me
Even if you don't like me, you know me

무플보단 악플이 좋아
I like hate comments more than no comments
무-none; 악- bad

난 널 몰라
I don't know you
But you know my name
But you know my name

I love I love I love myself
I love I love I love myself
I know I know I know myself
Ya playa haters you should love yourself
Brr

I wanna get 잠 time
I wanna get sleep time
쉴 틈 없이 받는 spotlight
Without a chance to rest, we're receiving spotlight
쉴- resting; 틈- period, time
Ahh you wanna be my life?
굶주린 놈들은 내 총알받이나 해
Those who are starving, just be my human shield
굶주린- starving, hungry; 총알- bullets
곱게 접해 내 멋대로 도배된
Contacted softly and got spammed on my accord
곱게- nicely, softly; 접해- touched, contacted; 도배된- roasted
무대로 연행 다 결백 (okay)
Haul to the stage all innocent okay
무대- stage; 연행- haul; 결백- innocent
But 만족 못해 절대 여기에
But I can't be satisfied just being here
나 올라 저 위에 높게 높게 높게
I'm climbing up there, high high high
그래 방식은 다르지
That's right, my method is different
방식- method; 다르다- to be different
굽씹어도 가는 길
I take on the road no matter what
굽씹어도- no matter

한 땀씩 바느질
Sewing stich by stich
땀-sweat; 씩- each; 바느질- sewing

못 할 거면 매듭지어
If you're not able, put an end to it
매듭지어- knot, end

이젠 안 돼 가능이
There is no possibility
안 돼- wrong; 가능이- possibility

포기라는 발음이
Of pronouncing "failure"
포기라는- giving up; 발음- pronunciation

I love ma rule 내 bro 들과 하는 일
I love ma rule, the work that I do with my bros

그들만의 리그의 플레이어
Players in a league of their own

난 그 위 감독이 될 테니
I'll become the supervisor above them
위- above; 감독- director; 테니- seems

다 될 대로해
So come what may

1VERSE 에 이어 난 더 큰 그림을 그릴 테니
Following 1VERSE, I'll draw a bigger picture
그림- picture; 그릴 테니- would draw

평생
For the rest of your life,

그 위치에서 쭉 외쳐봐라
Continue screaming from that position
위치(에서)- (from)position; 쭉- straight; 외쳐봐라- try screaming

'Dream come true'
명예와 부는 그게 아냐 you
Honor and wealth isn't that you
명예(와)- honor(and); 부는- wealth

다 결국 내 발바닥 츄
Everyone chu on my foot sole after all
결국- result; 발바닥- sole

클릭해, 난 cat 다 mouse
Click, I'm cat, everyone's mouse

골라 X 쳐 like kaws
I choose and put an X like kaws
난 내년 입주 ma house
I move in next year ma house
내년- next year; 입주- enter

에서 내 brick 과 high five
And high five with my brick
눈뜨고 봐라 내 야망
Open your eyes and look at my ambition
눈뜨고- open eyes; 야망- ambition

귀 대고 들어라
Lean in your ears and listen
귀 대고- perk ears; 들어라- listen

처음이자 마지막이 될 말
This will be the first and final words
마지막- final


I love I love I love myself
I love I love I love myself
I know I know I know myself
Ya playa haters you should love yourself
Brr

Back back to the basic
Microphone check
Call me 뱁새 혹은 쎈캐
Call me a crow tit or badass
그래 rap game 에 난 대인배
Yes in this rap game,
되게 해이해졌던
I'm the generous one
해이해졌던- became generous, happy

Rap man 들을 갱생하는 게
To rehabilitate the rap man who began to slack
갱생- rebirth

내 첫 번째의 계획 hashtag
Is my first plan hashtag
계획- plan

Sucka betta run 인스타 속 gang gang
Sucka betta run gang gang in insta

그건 걔 인생이고
That's their life,
걔- their, your, her, etc.
내 인생은 뭐 매일매일
My life is just day by day
Payday, paycheck 손목 위엔 rolex
Payday, paycheck, rolex on my wrist
Click clack to the bang bang
Click clack to the pow
I'm so high 어딜 넘봐
I'm so high; how dare you covet
니가 도움닫기를 해도 손 닿기엔 높아
Even if you get help, it's too high for you to reach
도움- help; 손- hand; 닿기- reach; 높아- high
꽤나 먼 차이 절대 못 봐
The difference is pretty big, you can't see it
꽤나- quite; 먼- far; 차이- difference; 절대- absolutely; 못 봐- can't see
너의 똥차들의 콩깍지를
Your shitty car delusions
똥차들- poop cars; 콩깍지- delusions
몽땅 벗겨놓은 다음
after all shattering
몽땅- all; 벗겨놓- throw away; 다음- after
죄다 농락한 뒤 송장이 된
And once everyone's done toying with them
죄다- all; 송장이- debt, invoice, corpse

면상 위를 so fly
면상- face
So fly above your face that became a corpse
Click clack to the bang, you and you
쉽게 얻은 게 하나도 없음에 늘 감사하네
I'm always thankful, for not earning anything so easily
쉽게- easily; 얻은- getting; 게- thing; 늘- always
니 인생이 어중간한 게 왜 내 탓이야
Why is it my fault, that your life is noncommittal
어중간한- noncommitted; 탓- fault
계속 그렇게 살아줘 적당하게
Keep on living like that vaguely

계속- keep; 적당하게- vaguely

미안한데 앞으로 난 더 벌
Sorry but continue to look
앞으로- in the future
건데 지켜봐줘
지켜봐줘- care for, earn
Because I'm gonna earn more from now
부디 제발 건강하게
By all means please healthily
부디- please; 제발- please; 건강하게- healthily

I love I love I love myself
I love I love I love myself
I know I know I know myself
Ya playa haters you should love yourself
Brr

I love I love I love myself
I love I love I love myself
I know I know I know myself
Ya playa haters you should love yourself
Brr

Love K-pop and K-dramas? Check out our other great books to help you learn Korean with Korean pop culture:

Can't Stop Korean with K-pop
Learn Korean with Girls' Generation
Learn Korean thru K-pop
Learn Korean with Big Bang
Learn Korean with Korean Dramas: The Heirs

All available on Amazon.com

94037505R00061

Made in the USA
Columbia, SC
18 April 2018